REVISE E
Geog
Evolvin
For the li   ching 2012

Series Consult
Authors: David Flint, Rob Bircher and Kirsty Taylor

A note from the publisher

In order to ensure that this resource offers high-quality support for the associated Edexcel qualification, it has been through a review process by the awarding body to confirm that it fully covers the teaching and learning content of the specification or part of a specification at which it is aimed, and demonstrates an appropriate balance between the development of subject skills, knowledge and understanding, in addition to preparation for assessment.

While the publishers have made every attempt to ensure that advice on the qualification and its assessment is accurate, the official specification and associated assessment guidance materials are the only authoritative source of information and should always be referred to for definitive guidance.

Edexcel examiners have not contributed to any sections in this resource relevant to examination papers for which they have responsibility.

No material from an endorsed resource will be used verbatim in any assessment set by Edexcel.

Endorsement of a resource does not mean that the resource is required to achieve this Edexcel qualification, nor does it mean that it is the only suitable material available to support the qualification, and any resource lists produced by the awarding body shall include this and other appropriate resources.

For the full range of Pearson revision titles across GCSE, BTEC and AS Level visit:

www.pearsonschools.co.uk/revise

ALWAYS LEARNING   PEARSON

Contents

1-to-1 page match with the Revision Workbook ISBN 9781446905388

> ✓ Make sure you know which topics you have studied – you only need to revise these.

A small bit of small print
Edexcel publishes Sample Assessment Material and the Specification on its website. This is the official content and this book should be used in conjunction with it. The questions in *Now try this* have been written to help you practise every topic in the book. Remember: the real exam questions may not look like this.

Target grade ranges
Target grade ranges are quoted in this book for some of the questions. Students targeting this grade range should be aiming to get most of the marks available. Students targeting a higher grade should be aiming to get all the marks available.

Moving tectonic plates

The Earth is made up of a series of layers which are a bit like the layers of an onion. There are three main layers.

Crust – made from thin layers of **tectonic plates**

Mantle – divided into solid upper part and semi-liquid lower part, which can flow

Core – consists of a liquid outer core and solid inner core

How convection currents cause plate movement

1 The core heats the molten rock in the mantle to create a **convection current**.

2 Heated rock from the mantle rises to the Earth's surface.

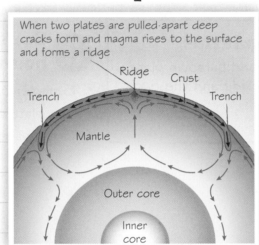

When two plates are pulled apart deep cracks form and magma rises to the surface and forms a ridge

Ridge

Crust

Trench

Trench

Mantle

Outer core

Inner core

3 At the surface the convection current moves the tectonic plates in the crust.

4 Molten rock cools and flows back to the core to be reheated.

Worked example

F-E

Which of the following best describes the differences between oceanic and continental crust? **(1 mark)**

✓ **A** Continental crust is thicker but less dense than oceanic crust.

☐ **B** Continental crust is thicker and more dense than oceanic crust.

☐ **C** Oceanic crust is thicker but less dense than continental crust.

☐ **D** Oceanic crust is thicker and more dense than continental crust.

EXAM ALERT!

This is a classic example of a question that many students get wrong. With multiple choice questions make sure you read all four options carefully before making your choice.

Students have struggled with exam questions similar to this – **be prepared!**

ResultsPlus

Now try this

1 Identify the **three** main layers that make up the Earth. **(3 marks)**

Make sure you name all **three** layers as a list.

2 Briefly explain what happens when two plates are pulled apart. **(2 marks)**

Plate boundaries, volcanoes and earthquakes

There are three main types of plate boundaries.

1 Destructive plate boundaries

- **Example:** Nazca Plate and South American Plate
- Two plates collide, one plate flows beneath another (**subduction**)
- Many earthquakes and volcanoes

Collision plate boundaries

- **Example:** Indo-Australian and Eurasian plates
- Two continental plates collide and the two plates buckle
- Many earthquakes

2 Constructive plate boundaries

- **Example:** Eurasian and North American plates
- Rising **convection currents** pull crust apart forming volcanic ridge, e.g. Mid-Atlantic Ridge

3 Conservative plate boundaries

- **Example:** San Andreas Fault, California
- Two plates slide past each other
- Earthquakes

Main tectonic plates

This is a diagram of the global tectonic plates. It shows the three main types of plate boundaries and the direction of the plate movement, as well as the collision boundary.

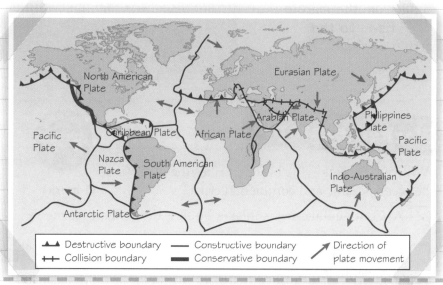

Worked example

Outline how a tsunami is formed.   **(2 marks)**

A tsunami can be triggered when an earthquake or a volcanic eruption happens at sea. The movement of the plates makes all of the water on top of this part of the seabed rise up. This creates two blocks of water which move in opposite directions, away from the epicentre, as huge waves.

Now try this

Make sure you spell the names of the plates correctly when you refer to them.

1 Describe what happens at a destructive plate boundary. **(4 marks)**

2 Identify **three** destructive plate margins in the world. **(3 marks)**

Volcanic and earthquake hazards

The amount of damage and devastation caused by tectonic hazards depends on various factors.

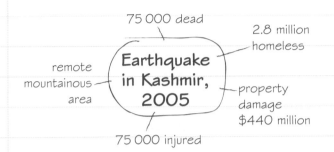

75 000 dead
2.8 million homeless
remote mountainous area
Earthquake in Kashmir, 2005
property damage $440 million
75 000 injured

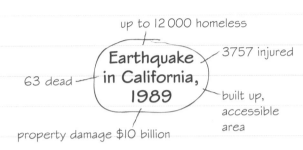

up to 12 000 homeless
3757 injured
63 dead
Earthquake in California, 1989
built up, accessible area
property damage $10 billion

Shield volcanoes:

- are found on constructive plate boundaries
- are formed by eruptions of thin, runny lava which flows a long way before it solidifies
- have gently sloping sides and a wide base
- contain basaltic magma which is very hot with low **silica** and gas content
- erupt frequently but not violently.

Composite volcanoes:

- are found on destructive plate boundaries
- are formed by eruptions of viscous, sticky lava and ash that don't flow far
- have steep sloping sides and a narrow base
- made up of layers of thick lava and ash
- contain andesitic magma which is less hot but contains lots of **silica** and gas
- erupt infrequently but violently, including pyroclastic flows (mix of ash, gases and rock).

 **Worked example**

Explain why some earthquakes cause more damage and loss of life than others. **(4 marks)**

HIGHER B-A

Some earthquakes cause more loss of life and damage because the severity of each earthquake may vary. When earthquakes are more powerful, more people and buildings are affected. Some places are also more vulnerable to earthquakes. For example, in parts of Pakistan and Kashmir there is very little money to build earthquake-proof homes and train people in what to do in an earthquake. These are some of the reasons why 75 000 people were killed in Kashmir in 2005. By contrast, the Loma Pieta earthquake in California in 1989 only killed 63 people because California has money to build homes and offices which are more resistant to earthquakes and people have regular earthquake practice drills.

There are two scales used to measure the **magnitude** (strength) of an earthquake. The Richter Scale measures the **energy** released. The magnitude increases 10 fold as you move up the scale. The Mercalli Scale measures the **effects** or impacts and is measured in roman numerals I to XII.

⬅ Explain all your points **clearly** and give examples.

Now try this

1 Explain why some volcanic eruptions have a greater impact than others. **(4 marks)**

 HIGHER B

2 Describe what a pyroclastic flow is. **(3 marks)**

 FOUNDN D-C

Managing earthquake and volcanic hazards

Earthquakes and volcanoes are difficult to manage because they are difficult to predict. Managing these hazards is based on preparation and prediction.

The difficulties of predicting earthquakes and volcanoes

We do not know...

👎 when it will happen
👎 exactly where it will happen
👎 how big it will be
👎 what other impacts it may have
👎 how many people live there.

What can help us predict earthquakes and volcanoes?

Look out for...

👍 animals and birds moving away from the area
👍 an increase in gas emissions
👍 an increase in soil temperature
👍 the volcano swelling
👍 an increase in small earthquakes
👍 water in ponds getting warmer.

What is needed after an earthquake or volcanic eruption?

- Trained volunteers to help the injured people and to clear away the debris.
- Clean water to prevent the spread of disease.
- Food because often shops, towns, roads and farms have been damaged.
- Radio communication because phones will often not work.
- Medical help to care for the injured people.
- A plan to evacuate the area if needed.

Buildings in earthquake areas

How to strengthen a building

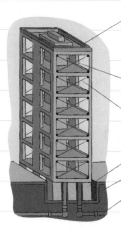

Installing a ring beam (band of concrete) at roof level to stop walls falling outwards

Very strong framework in skyscrapers

Strengthening walls

Making foundations from rubber and steel which can move slightly

Digging deeper foundations

Reinforce gas and water pipes so they do not break

Worked example

B-A

Describe **two** differences in the ways in which buildings are made earthquake resistant in the developed and developing world.   **(4 marks)**

In the developed world, there is more money available to spend on making buildings earthquake resistant, for example by using rubber and steel foundations which can move slightly. Another difference is that buildings in the developing world are more likely to be made from timber. A cheap way to make these buildings stronger is to add timber diagonal braces which reduce movement.

> Make sure you include **two** separate ways in your answer.

Now try this

1 Give **two** clues which tell you when a volcano may erupt.
   (2 marks)

2 Outline some of the plans that can be made to deal with the after-effects of a volcanic eruption.   **(3 marks)**

Earthquake case study

You need to be able to evaluate the role of immediate responses and relief efforts for a named tectonic event. On 12 January 2010, a powerful earthquake measuring 7.0 M struck the country of Haiti near the capital, Port-au-Prince.

Data file: the Haiti earthquake

- 316 000 people died.
- Over 250 000 homes and 30 000 offices and factories destroyed or so badly damaged they had to be demolished.
- A nursing school and a midwifery school were destroyed along with the presidential palace.
- Roads blocked by rubble.

Primary impacts

- Injured and dead trapped under rubble.
- People sleeping in the streets for fear of more earthquakes.
- Mortuaries unable to deal with the vast numbers of dead people. Mass graves dug to bury people.
- Phone and power lines down.
- Streets blocked by huge piles of rubble from collapsed buildings.

The relief effort

By 2012:
- 80% of the rubble has been cleared.
- Only 18% of the required homes had been built.
- 350 000 people still living in tents.
- There is a shortage of safe, clean water.
- Only 111 000 out of the 125 000 shelters planned had been built.
- Not all of the money promised in aid had been sent, making recovery difficult.

Worked example

FOUND'N C

Using an example, describe the immediate responses to an earthquake.   **(4 marks)**

There was a major earthquake in Haiti in January 2010. The immediate response was quite slow partly because the transport and communications were so badly affected and Haiti is a very poor country. The government and charities tried to supply tents, blankets, food and clean water to survivors but the relief effort was uncoordinated and survivors slept in the streets for weeks until camps were set up. It took over 3 days to reach some of the smaller towns affected. Rescue teams tried to find the injured and dead but met with limited success.

Now try this

1 Give **two** primary impacts of an earthquake you have studied.   **(2 marks)**

2 Using examples, compare the primary impacts of different earthquakes.   **(6 marks)**

Start by underlining the most important words in the question.

Volcanic eruptions

If people live near volcanoes, eruptions can be very destructive to property and threaten lives. Even if eruptions occur in remote areas, their effect can be very damaging. You need to know the primary and secondary economic and social impacts of one volcanic event.

The Montserrat volcano, 1995

- The volcano had been dormant since the 17th century.
- The eruption sent out large amounts of ash and lava, including pyroclastic flows.
- Over 6500 people out of 10000 left the island.
- The whole island was affected.
- The eruption had a devastating economic and social effect.

Laki, Iceland, 1783–84

- The eruption was huge, occurring in a remote area where people could not escape.
- Poisonous gases caused vegetation and subsequently animals to die, leading to the death through starvation of over 25% of Iceland's population.
- No aid from other countries was possible.
- A huge dust cloud covered much of Europe and led to poor summers for years afterwards.

Eyjafjallajökull, Iceland, 2010

- The eruption occurred under a glacier, which caused ice to melt.
- This resulted in an ash cloud.
- Magma inside the volcano turned the water to steam which resulted in an explosion, causing the magma to shatter and explode into tiny fragments.
- Caused massive disruption to air travel and air routes over 20 European countries were closed for several weeks.

Worked example

Explain the primary and secondary impacts of a volcanic event you have studied. **(6 marks)**

The volcanic eruption in Montserrat in 1995 had many primary and secondary impacts. Primary impacts included the destruction of Montserrat's capital city, Plymouth, as it was covered in ash; the destruction of most of the island's crops due to ash and the evacuation of people from the southern part of the island (where the volcano is) to safer areas on the island or overseas. Another primary impact was the destruction of forests by fires ignited by gases from the volcano. The secondary impacts include the fact that half of the original population of Montserrat has permanently left the island which has had a huge impact on the economy of the island, as well as socially. Another secondary impact is that Plymouth has become a 'ghost town'. Before the eruption, most services were located in Plymouth. Since then, some but not all have been relocated in other parts of the island.

Now try this

1 Outline **one** preparation that could be made by people living close to a dormant volcano in case of eruption. **(2 marks)**

2 Describe **two** primary impacts of a volcanic event you have studied. **(4 marks)**

Past climate change

A variety of **natural** causes are thought to have affected global temperatures and patterns of rainfall. You should be able to explain some of these natural causes.

This graph shows how the Earth's temperature has cooled and warmed over 450 000 years. It demonstrates **long-term** temperature changes due to natural causes.

The data for this graph comes from ice cores and fossils. **Ice cores** are cylinders of ice obtained by drilling through glaciers 3 km deep in ice up to 500 000 years old.

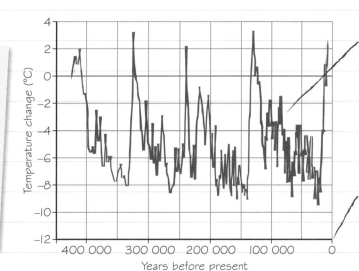

When the temperature is cooler for longer periods, more of the Earth is covered in ice. This is called an Ice Age or **glacial**.

This is now! We are in a warmer period or an **interglacial**.

Some natural causes of climate change

- The Earth's orbit changes a small amount once every 100 000 years. These are known as **Milankovitch cycles**.
- The amount of energy radiated from the Sun changes over an 11-year cycle.
- Volcanic eruptions pump ash dust into the atmosphere causing a cooling effect.
- Large asteroid collisions can cause cooling as material blocks out the Sun. Asteroids hitting the Earth can cause huge fires which release massive amounts of CO_2 which subsequently has a warming effect.
- Ocean current changes can cause cooling and warming. In the UK, we have a warm and wet climate because of warm Atlantic currents. Sometimes the current shifts and we get a cooler climate for a short period of time.

Worked example

Which **one** of the following statements about past climate change is correct? **(1 mark)**

☐ A Average global temperatures have stayed roughly constant for the last 450 000 years.

☐ B Average global temperatures have been steadily warming for the last 450 000 years.

☐ C Average global temperatures have been steadily cooling for the last 450 000 years.

☑ D Average global temperatures have shown patterns of warm, cool and cold periods for the last 450 000 years.

Now try this

1 Describe **one** natural cause of climate change. **(2 marks)**

2 Describe what is meant by the term 'Ice Age'. **(2 marks)**

The impact of climate change

Past climate change has had an impact on plant life, animal life and on people. You need to know an historical example of the impact of climate change on people.

Impact on people – The Little Ice Age

A colder period in northern Europe starting in the 15th century and lasting to the mid 19th century.

Crops did not grow well which meant less productivity and less food for people.

The Little Ice Age

The winters were very cold and the summers short.

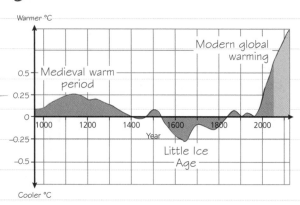

Causes

Could be caused by:

- fewer sunspots
- volcanic ash in the atmosphere.

Unlikely to be caused by:

- humans because not enough people or industry to cause climate change.

Evidence

- diaries, newspapers and paintings
- the tree rings in old trees are thinner during cold years.

The impact of climate change on megafauna

| Megafauna, such as mammoths, giant beavers and sabre-toothed tigers, had evolved during the Ice Age. | → | The Ice Age ended and temperatures rose 5°C in 10 000 years. | → | The megafauna couldn't adapt to the warmer climate and became extinct. Hunting by early humans could also have been a factor in their extinction. |

Worked example

Describe **one** impact of a colder period, such as the Little Ice Age, on human activity. **(2 marks)**

Because the Little Ice Age shortened the growing seasons for crops, it meant people could grow less food so they went hungry.

EXAM ALERT!

Another way to answer this question would be to give two shorter points, for example, '... because of the shorter growing seasons for crops and because cod migrated away from fishing areas there was less food so people went hungry'.

Students have struggled with exam questions similar to this – **be prepared!**

Now try this

1 Outline **one** reason why many scientists think climate change led to the extinction of megafauna.

(2 marks)

2 Describe **two** sources of evidence for climate change in the last 10 000 years. **(4 marks)**

Present and future climate change

Most scientists agree that humans are changing the Earth's climate. You need to know how **greenhouse gases** are produced and how this may lead to the greenhouse effect.

1 Carbon dioxide (CO_2) and **methane** (CH_4) are greenhouse gases linked to human activity.

2 The rise in greenhouse gas emissions matches the start of the Industrial Revolution.

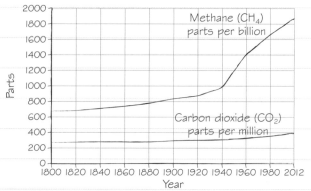

3 Current levels of CO_2 are thought to be at their highest for at least 650 000 years.

4 Current levels of CH_4 are thought to be at their highest for at least 900 000 years.

5 Methane is 21 times more potent than carbon dioxide.

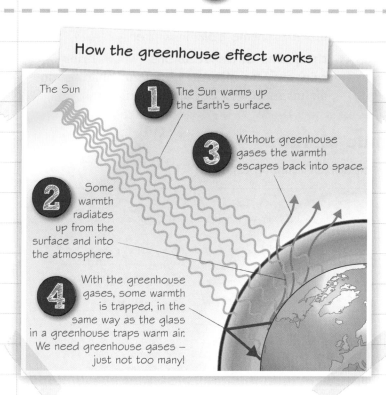

How the greenhouse effect works

The Sun

1 The Sun warms up the Earth's surface.

2 Some warmth radiates up from the surface and into the atmosphere.

3 Without greenhouse gases the warmth escapes back into space.

4 With the greenhouse gases, some warmth is trapped, in the same way as the glass in a greenhouse traps warm air. We need greenhouse gases – just not too many!

Greenhouse gases

As a country develops, the amount of greenhouse gases it releases into the atmosphere is increased.

More **carbon dioxide** is produced because:

- there is more industry, e.g. steel and cement making
- more energy is needed so more fossil fuels are burned
- transport increases so more oil is burned as petrol and diesel
- land is needed so there is **deforestation** (trees are often burned).

More **methane** is produced because there is more demand for meat so there are more farm animals.

Worked example

Describe **one** human activity that is thought to contribute to climate change. **(2 marks)**

Burning coal for electricity because it releases CO_2 which is a greenhouse gas linked to global warming.

Now try this

1 Wind power generation, steel production, solar power generation and recycling are all types of human activity. Which one is a major source of greenhouse gases? **(1 mark)**

2 State **two** of the main greenhouse gases associated with human activity. **(2 marks)**

9

Climate change challenges

The UK's climate is affected by global and local factors. You need to learn these, to be able to describe some climate projections and consider how the UK's climate might change.

The UK climate

The climate of the UK is mild (cool) and wet. It's described as **temperate maritime**. Several factors impact on the UK's climate.

- **Latitude** affects how much Sun the UK gets and how strong it is during the different seasons.
- The North Atlantic current (or drift) keeps the UK warmer than other places of the same latitude.
- Air masses bring weather conditions with them from where they originated. The UK is affected by five air masses.
- The **prevailing winds** are from the Atlantic Ocean in the south west. They pick up moisture from the sea and often bring rain to the UK.

UK climate change

Possible changes to the UK's climate include:

- average temperature rise
- less predictable rainfall patterns with drier summers
- changing seasons – possibly longer summers and more extreme cold in winter.

Changes will happen because:

- the North Atlantic current is likely to move which will probably reduce sea temperatures and bring less rainfall
- more air masses will come from the north, bringing more storms and perhaps more extreme cold in winter
- the **paths of depressions** (which bring rain) may be altered by these changes in air masses and ocean currents.

Predicting the effects of climate change

Scientists use CO_2 levels to estimate the impact of climate change:

In 2008, global CO_2 reached 380 ppm (parts per million).

→ If concentrations go over 550 ppm, predictions are that global temperature rises will be 6°C or more.

→ Possible consequences:
- millions of people would lose their homes due to sea-level rises
- changes to world weather patterns would cause droughts and storms leading to famines and disasters
- animal and plant species would not be able to adapt fast enough to the changes.

→ If concentrations stay under 550 ppm, predictions are that global temperature rises will not go over 2°C.

→ Possible consequences:
- sea level might rise by up to 1 m, causing coastal flooding
- more storms and hurricanes
- some species may become extinct, others would shift to new zones.

Worked example

HIGHER C-B

State **two** challenges for people in the UK that could result from an average global temperature rise of 2°C. **(2 marks)**.

One challenge could be the possible flooding of towns on the coast; another might be the increased threat of drought from less reliable rainfall.

Now try this

HIGHER A-A*

Explain how the future climate of the UK is likely to be affected by global climate change. **(6 marks)**

Remember these are only predictions! One of the problems is that climate is affected by many different factors acting at the same time.

Climate change in the UK

The UK is a developed country, which means it can raise money to spend defending itself from the **impacts** of climate change. You need to examine the possible economic and environmental impacts of future climate change on the UK.

Environmental impacts

- Sea level rise will lead to the loss of coastal land and increased erosion. Risk of low-lying cities flooding, e.g. London.
- More severe storms and longer summer droughts.
- Changes to fishing industries if fish species move to different waters.
- Ecosystem change could mean some plant and animal species move into new areas and new (invasive) species emerge.
- Warmer temperatures could encourage diseases such as malaria.

Economic impacts

- An increase in refugees from other countries hit hard by climate change coming to the UK.
- Warmer weather may mean farmers can grow different crops and enjoy a longer growing season.
- Hotter summers could mean more people have holidays in the UK (so less air travel overseas).
- Damage to cities such as London from flooding would be extremely expensive and very disruptive.
- Cost of protecting places from flooding will be expensive and in some cases not practical.
- Housing design might need to be altered so that less water is wasted and higher temperatures are dealt with.

Worked example

FOUNDN E-D

Explain some of the possible economic impacts of climate change on the UK. **(4 marks)**

Climate change in the UK could cause flooding in London. This would prevent businesses making money and it would cost a lot to repair the flood damage. Climate change could also mean less rainfall, causing drought. It would cost money to move water around the country to supply those areas which need it. However, if the climate was warmer, that might encourage tourism which would make more money for the UK.

Some of the effects will be positive as well as negative and much depends on how big the increase in temperatures is.

Now try this

FOUNDN G-E

1 Which **one** of these statements is **not** linked to a possible **economic** impact of climate change in the UK?

☐ A Rising sea levels increase coastal erosion.

☐ B Less snow for Scottish ski resorts.

☐ C More tropical diseases in the UK.

☐ D Some species, such as the black grouse, may become extinct. **(1 mark)**

2 Explain why developed countries are likely to be able to deal with the impact of climate change better than lower-income countries. **(4 marks)**

HIGHER B-A

Explain all your points **clearly** and give examples.

Climate change in Bangladesh

You need to examine the possible economic and environmental impacts of future climate change on a developing country. Bangladesh is a low-lying country that is already experiencing many problems from coastal and river flooding. It has a very large and very poor population which makes it extremely vulnerable to climate change.

Environmental impacts

- River flooding (which is already severe) would become worse from heavier rains and sea level rise.
- Tropical storms could become even more frequent and may move further inland, doing more damage.
- The dry season is already getting longer and this could cause more droughts.

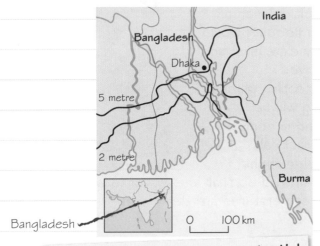

Land that could be lost to potential sea-level rises in Bangladesh

Economic impacts

- A small rise in sea level (just a few cm) could massively reduce Bangladesh's farmland and agricultural output.
- More river flooding would mean more damage to people's homes and more disruption to lives and the economy.
- More intense tropical storms and storms spreading inland would increase damage to homes, lives and infrastructure.
- Bangladesh has a large, fast-growing population; many are farmers who need land to work.
- The cost of protecting homes and businesses from flooding is more than people or the government can afford.
- Coastal flooding damages farmland by making the land too salty to grow crops.
- Shrimp farming is very important but rising sea temperatures may damage this form of aquaculture.
- Increased flooding will increase the spread of water-borne diseases.

Worked example

A

Explain the possible **economic impacts** of climate change on a named developing country. **(4 marks)**.

When floods happen in Bangladesh, businesses have to close so they lose money. When farmland is flooded by the sea, it leaves salt on the land. This can make the soil useless for growing crops so the farmers have nothing to sell. Climate change could increase the incidences of flooding which would make the economic problems worse. Building flood defences to try and help will be very expensive and Bangladesh is too poor to pay for what is needed.

Now try this

1 Using examples, outline some of the possible **environmental impacts** of future climate change on a named country or region.
(3 marks)

2 Describe how climate change can have **both** positive and negative impacts for people. **(4 marks)**

Bangladesh is a **developing** country, which means it does not have the **infrastructure** and funding to protect itself from climate change unlike a more developed country, such as the UK.

Distribution of biomes

You need to be able to define the terms **ecosystem** and **biome**. You also need to know the location of the world's biomes and how they are connected to climate.

Definitions

Ecosystem: a grouping of plants and animals that interact with each other and their local environment.

Biome: a large ecosystem – a grouping of plants and animals over a large area of the Earth.

Coniferous biome
Coniferous forests are at higher latitudes where the Sun's rays are weak. Trees are adapted to the cold with needle-like leaves.

Deciduous biome
Deciduous forests have high rainfall and there are seasonal variations in the Sun's rays. Trees lose their leaves in the cool winters.

Tundra biome
The **tundra** is within the Arctic Circle. The Sun gives little heat here and there is little rainfall. Only tough, short grasses survive.

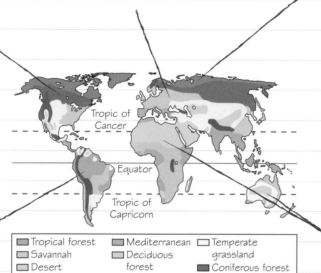

Tropic of Cancer

Equator

Tropic of Capricorn

☐ Tropical forest ☐ Mediterranean ☐ Temperate grassland
☐ Savannah ☐ Deciduous forest ☐ Coniferous forest
☐ Desert ☐ Mountain ☐ Tundra

Desert biome
Deserts are close to the tropics of Cancer and Capricorn. This is where hot dry air sinks down to the Earth's surface and the Sun's rays are concentrated making it very hot in the day.

Tropical biome
Tropical rainforests are mostly found either side of the Equator. The temperature is hot and there is heavy rainfall.

Worked example

Explain how climate controls the distribution of biomes, such as tropical rainforests. **(4 marks)**

Climate plays an important role in the distribution of biomes, such as tropical rainforests, around the world. Areas closest to the Equator, where the Sun's rays are most direct, have hot temperatures. Further north or south of the Equator, there is less sunlight and the Sun's rays are weaker so temperatures are colder.

Sunlight, temperature and rainfall affect the type and amount of plants that can grow in different places. Tropical rainforests contain the greatest variety and density of plant growth because they are located in regions which are hot and where there is plenty of rainfall. In contrast, tundra regions are cold and dry which means that only tough, short grasses can survive.

Now try this

1 In which of the following biomes is the UK found?

☐ **A** Tropical rainforest.
☐ **B** Mediterranean.
☐ **C** Deciduous forest.
☐ **D** Coniferous forest.
(1 mark)

2 Using the map, describe the distribution of the tundra biome.
(2 marks)

Remember that tropical rainforests are mostly found either side of the Equator. Try to include specific examples to support your points.

A life-support system

The biosphere is the Earth's life-support system. It provides humans with a wide range of essential goods.

A life-support system

It regulates the gases that make up the **atmosphere** – plants absorb carbon dioxide and produce oxygen for us to breathe in.

It regulates the **water cycle** – plants slow the flow of water to rivers and filter water to make it clean.

Biosphere – what it does for us

It keeps **soil** healthy for plants to grow – new nutrients are provided by rotting plant material.

Goods provided by the biosphere

Food	Medicines	Raw materials
Fish	Vitamin	Timber
Meat	Plants used to make medicines, e.g. quinine from bark, St John's wort, periwinkle	Bamboo
Fruits		Rubber
Nuts		Water
Berries		Oil and gas store carbon

The pressure to feed large populations has meant that natural vegetation has been replaced with farmland to grow crops such as wheat, corn and rice. Very few communities survive solely on food from the biosphere.

Worked example

Using examples, explain why the biosphere is important for humans.   **(6 marks)**

The biosphere regulates the gases in the atmosphere. This means that plants absorb carbon dioxide that animals (including humans) breathe out and produce oxygen which animals breathe in keeping a balance. The biosphere also maintains the health of the soil through decomposing plants providing the nutrients for new plant life. This provides humans with food directly, such as fruit and nuts and indirectly, through providing grazing for animals that humans eat. People also use raw materials from the biosphere in various ways. For example, wood is used to make furniture or build houses, rubber is used in the manufacturing of many products and oil and gas provide energy to heat people's homes and run their cars. The biosphere also provides humans with medicines such as quinine and St John's wort. Finally, the biosphere regulates the water cycle, providing humans with the clean water that is essential for life.

Now try this

1 Identify **two** biosphere **goods** from this list: meat, fruit, nylon, oxygen, leaves.   **(2 marks)**
2 Outline **two** reasons why humans should look after the biosphere.   **(2 marks)**

Threats to the biosphere

In many parts of the world, the biosphere is being degraded by human activity. You need to be able to give an example of how people are destroying the biosphere.

Degradation of the biosphere by human activity

Ways humans destroy the biosphere directly	Ways humans destroy the biosphere indirectly
Deforestation Mining Quarrying Farming Overfishing	Pollution and climate change causing (among other things): • sea temperature rise • **seawater acidification** • melting of polar ice caps • changes in amounts of rainfall • **treeline** changes • stress within ecosystems due to rapid change

Reasons for rainforest destruction

1 Timber used for buildings, furniture and fuel.

2 Creation of agricultural land for growing crops or grazing animals.

3 Mining and quarrying of minerals for construction industry, jewellery, etc.

4 Transport routes.

5 Building human settlements.

6 Building dams and power stations to provide power.

This is only an extract from an answer. To do well you would need to add other developed examples of ways people have destroyed the rainforest, e.g. agriculture, road building and housing for a growing population.

Worked example

Explain the role of human activity in the destruction of tropical rainforest.

(6 marks)

Humans have destroyed tropical rainforest in many ways and for different **reasons**. Some of these reasons are economic – to make money from the resources of the forest, which is necessary as most countries with tropical rainforests are quite poor. Trees are cut down and sold to make furniture. Forest is also cleared for mining and quarrying so people can make money from the minerals found. An example of this is the Grande Carajas development programme in Brazil which mines iron and aluminium from huge areas where forest once stood.

Now try this

1 Define the term 'ecosystem degradation'.   **(2 marks)**

2 Outline **one** reason why tropical rainforest is being cut down (deforestation) in some parts of the world.   **(2 marks)**

Management of the biosphere

Different management methods are used to conserve and use the biosphere sustainably. You need to know one example of biosphere conservation at a global scale and one at a national or local scale.

RAMSAR (named after city in Iran)

Scale: global – 168 countries have signed up to it
Started: 1971
What it conserves: 2.05 million km² of wetlands around the world
Why: wetlands provide a rich **biodiversity** with many rare species
How it is threatened: population growth means wetlands are drained for farmland, also vulnerable to climate change
Management type: international treaty protects important wetlands by law.

Lalo Loor Dry Forest Reserve

Scale: local
Where: Ecuador
What it conserves: 500 acres of tropical rainforest
Why: almost untouched rainforest, home to large numbers of animals and plants
How it is threatened: clearance for soya production (this has happened in surrounding areas)
Management type: owner of the land has agreed a conservation deal, volunteers care for the land, run reforestation schemes and sustainable tourism to provide funds.

National Parks, UK

Scale: national
Started: 1951 (Peak District first one)
What it conserves: areas of natural beauty in the UK – 22 000 km² in 15 parks
Why: important for people's leisure, enjoyment and culture and to preserve wildlife and environment
How they are threatened: any development that would degrade the ecosystems, e.g. mining, construction, overdevelopment
Management type: each park has its own authority controlling any new development.

You might have studied different examples or places to the three examples given here. If you have, write up your own fact files, recording the following key information.

- What is being conserved?
- Why is it valuable?
- How is it threatened?
- Management type.

Worked example

Describe **one** way of conserving threatened environments.   **(2 marks)**

In the UK, National Parks conserve areas of special beauty. The area covered by the Parks is protected by law and any development that would harm the environment is not allowed.

Now try this

1 Describe **one** way in which humans try to protect ecosystems.   **(2 marks)**

2 CITES is the Convention on International Trade in Endangered Species. Outline the importance of international agreements such as these.   **(2 marks)**

Factors affecting biomes

There are local factors which have an influence on biomes. You need to know some of the different factors and explain how they can affect biomes.

Local factors affecting biomes

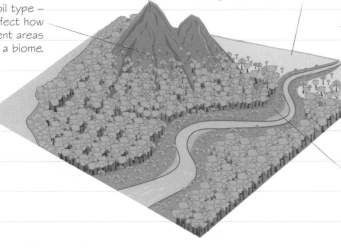

Altitude – different plants grow at different temperatures within the same biome. The higher the altitude the lower the temperature.

Rainfall – different types and amount of plants will grow in different parts of the biome depending on the amount of rainfall received. Inland areas are usually drier than coastal areas.

Rock and soil type – this can affect how fertile different areas are within a biome.

Distance from the sea – this can affect temperatures and especially amounts of rainfall within the same biome.

Drainage – swamps and bogs occur where drainage is poor. Fewer, more specialist plants grow in boggy areas.

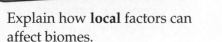

Worked example

HIGHER B-A

Explain how **local** factors can affect biomes. **(4 marks)**

Altitude is a local factor that can affect a biome. For example, there are glaciers in very high mountains near the Equator which is where you would expect tropical rainforest. Geology can affect a biome also. Limestone, for example, creates dry soil conditions because rainwater passes through the rock easily. This makes it difficult for trees to survive and so in a deciduous biome with limestone geology you wouldn't get many trees. Also aspect (the direction in which a slope faces) can affect the growing season, sunshine hours and so on.

Remember, whatever effect local factors have, humans can have the biggest impact on biomes. They can be responsible for clearing whole biome ecosystems and replacing them with something else.

EXAM ALERT!

Reading the question properly is essential – the word 'local' is emphasised here which tells you that this is the crucial part of the question. Do not write about global factors, such as latitude!

This was a real exam question that a lot of students struggled with – **be prepared!**

ResultsPlus

Now try this

HIGHER C-B

1 Outline why the east of England generally has less rain than the west of England. **(2 marks)**

2 Describe briefly how altitude can affect biomes. **(2 marks)**

FOUNDN D-C

Biosphere management tensions

You need to know what is meant by **sustainability** and some of the possible tensions between economic, social and environmental factors when managing a biosphere.

What is sustainability?

Sustainability is the ability to keep something going at the same rate or level. There are several key ideas when considering this as a Geographer. These are, that it:

- keeps going without using up natural resources
- doesn't require lots of money to keep it going
- meets the needs of people now and in the future without having a negative effect.

Sustainable biosphere management

👍 Ensures the ecosystem can recover quickly from any use.

👍 Prevents damage to the environment / ecosystem.

👍 Helps local people to benefit from their environment / ecosystem.

👍 Helps local people to understand why this management benefits them.

Possible tensions

1 Economic – individuals and communities often want to make as much money as possible, and may use the resources in the biosphere to do this. This provides tensions as it may damage or even destroy the environment in the long-term. This would mean it's not sustainable economically either, and it may harm or exploit other people now or in the future.

2 Social – to be socially sustainable something must not benefit one group / individual at the expense of another, including future generations. It also means consulting people on an equal basis. This can provide tensions because if everyone is to benefit, this may put the environment at risk. There are also economic tensions as some businesses may flourish at the expense of others.

3 Environmental – being environmentally sustainable means not harming natural resources so they cannot regenerate or continue in the long-term. There are economic tensions as people want to make as much money as possible, as well as social tensions as everyone wants to improve their standard of living.

Worked example

Using examples, describe some of the tensions between the **economy** and the **environment** when managing a biosphere. **(4 marks)**

There may be many tensions because in order to make money, people might end up destroying the environment. For example, there is a lot of money to be made from mining minerals which will benefit people and may help developing countries develop further. However, this will end up destroying the environment which will eventually harm people and means that it isn't economically sustainable anyway. Another cause of tension might be that it costs a lot of money to conserve an area which might negatively affect the country that is paying for it. Everyone needs to earn a living to survive and in some places it can be difficult to do this without harming the environment.

Now try this

1 Define the term 'economic sustainability'. **(2 marks)**

2 Using examples, describe some features of sustainable biosphere management. **(4 marks)**

The hydrological cycle

The Earth's water is always on the move.

The hydrological cycle

Key:

361 Water flow. The number of cubic kilometres of water that falls or rises each year.

13 Water store. The number of cubic kilometres of water that is stored.

1% of the Earth's water is stored in lakes, rivers, ground, atmosphere, marsh and vegetation

99% of the Earth's water is stored in oceans, ice caps and glaciers

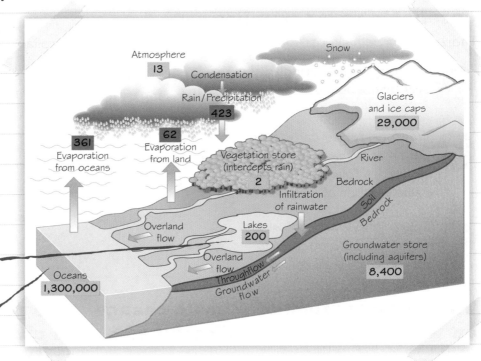

Overland flow (run-off)	Through flow	Groundwater flow
Rain falls onto the ground and flows on the surface to rivers and lakes.	Rainwater soaks into the soil (infiltration) and flows slowly through it to rivers.	Rainwater soaks into rocks below the soil. It moves slowly through the air spaces (pores) or flows along cracks and joints.

Worked example

Explain how human activity can affect infiltration. **(4 marks)**

When water soaks into the soil it is called infiltration. The water flows through the soil until it reaches a river. Human activity can affect this process. Building roads and other impermeable surfaces, such as offices and houses, decreases the rate of infiltration. This is because water flows along the impermeable surfaces rather than seeping into the soil. Human activity can also affect it in a different way, such as by planting trees which increases the infiltration of water into the soil to the roots.

Hydrological processes

Evaporation – as water heats up, it returns to the atmosphere as water vapour.

Condensation – water vapour forms into tiny water droplets as the air carrying it cools, sometimes forming visible clouds.

Precipitation – the tiny water droplets collide and grow until they fall to the ground as rain or snow.

Now try this

1 Describe how deforestation can affect water cycle processes. **(3 marks)**

2 Identify the **four** largest water stores in the water cycle. **(4 marks)**

Climate and water supplies

You need to know the impact of unreliable water supplies in a vulnerable area.

Unreliable water supplies

There are three main reasons why water supplies may be unreliable.

1 There may be distinct wet and dry seasons.

For example, the Sahel in Africa has a short wet season with high run-off so little water is stored.

2 Weather cycles can occur. So an area may get 3 or 5 dry years followed by the same number of wet years.

For example, the Sahel has had several **drought** years recently, leading to serious food shortages.

3 There is evidence of global warming and a continuing rise in temperatures.

Rising temperatures mean that dry places, such as the Sahel, may get drier and wet places, for example the UK, may get wetter.

The possible effect of climate change on water supplies in south-west USA

South-west USA is a very **arid** area with the Colorado River the main source of water, including the **irrigation** of crops.

Climate change may make the area even drier. In Las Vegas, 2002, 2004 and 2007 were drought years.

Restriction on taking water from the Colorado River, so less water for irrigation, meaning fewer crops and artificially created green areas.

Less water will create problems for the rapidly increasing population of this area. Arizona had a population increase of 25% between 2000 and 2010.

The possible effect of climate change on water supplies in Asia

Countries such as China, India and Vietnam depend on the water that comes from melting **glaciers** in the Himalayas.

Long-term impacts:
A warmer climate may melt the Himalayan glaciers leading to severely reduced water supplies.

Short-term impacts:
A warmer climate would increase glacier melt in the Himalayas leading to seasonal stress on agriculture, for example.

Worked example

Using examples, describe **two** impacts of unreliable water supplies on humans. **(4 marks)**

1 In Australia, unreliable water supplies have led to a fall in crop yields which has led to big increases in the price of food, such as bread.

2 Also, many Australian farmers are having to give up their land and livelihoods because the land is too dry to farm any more.

Explain all your points **clearly** and give examples.

Now try this

1 State **two** reasons why water supplies may be unreliable. **(2 marks)**

2 Using examples, describe **two** ways in which climate change can impact on the hydrological cycle. **(2 marks)**

Threats to the hydrological cycle

There are many human activities which impact on maintaining a healthy hydrological cycle.

Causes of river pollution

- Untreated sewage pumped into rivers can lead to serious diseases such as cholera and typhoid.
- **Fertilisers**, **pesticides** and **herbicides** from **intensive** agriculture can poison wildlife and affect water quality.
- Chemicals from factories can poison wildlife and affect water quality.
- Plastic bags and other waste which does not decay can kill wildlife, block water pipes and affect water quality.

Managing river pollution

- Sewage is treated before it can be pumped into rivers.
- Use of fertilisers and chemicals on the land is regulated to reduce pollution.
- Factories get rid of their waste products, such as chemicals, before they return water to the river. In the UK, the Environment Agency imposes heavy fines on any factory which does not do this.
- Plastic and other waste is sent to recycling centres rather than dumped in rivers.

Worked example

Using examples, explain ways in which human activities can disrupt water supplies. **(4 marks)** **B-A**

One way in which humans can disrupt water supply is through building reservoirs such as Lake Mead, the reservoir behind the Hoover Dam on the Colorado River in the USA. Reservoirs store large amounts of water in one place but mean that the water supply to areas further down the river is interrupted. This can have some positive effects, such as reducing flooding, but can also have negative effects, such as water shortages or harming ecosystems and wildlife.

Another way in which humans can disrupt water supply is through over-abstraction of natural water stores. Manufacturing processes that require the use of large quantities of water may access the groundwater store in drought-prone areas. This would leave the local people short of water as their own wells dry up.

Wherever possible, use proper geographical terminology – for example, 'over-abstraction'.

Now try this

C 1 State **three** causes of river pollution. **(3 marks)**

2 Give reasons why plastic bags in water supplies are a big problem. **(3 marks)**

Large-scale water management 1

'Water management' schemes try to deal with unreliable water supplies. You need to know an example of a large-scale water management scheme in the developed world.

Large-scale

These schemes:

- are expensive to build and maintain
- cover large areas
- are organised by local or national governments
- usually consist of dams and reservoirs being created.

The Colorado River

The Colorado River is managed on a **large scale**. There are benefits and disadvantages to it.

Benefits

👍 **Regulates** the flow of water – reduces summer flooding and winter drought.

👍 The **dams** generate electricity for towns, farms and factories.

👍 The lakes which form behind the dams store water which is used for **irrigation**.

👍 The stored water is also used to supply growing cities such as Las Vegas.

👍 There is a year-round supply of clean water for local US cities.

Disadvantages

👎 Land is lost when it is flooded to make lakes behind the dams.

👎 **Sediment** has built up behind the dams which affects the workings of **hydroelectric power** (HEP) generation.

👎 Less sediment flowing down the river has disrupted the habitat for native fish.

👎 Less sediment means sandbanks have shrunk so animal habitats are affected.

👎 Less water downstream in Mexico.

Worked example

Choose **one** large-scale water management project and examine its advantages and disadvantages. **(6 marks)**

The Hoover Dam and the Glen Canyon Dam built on the River Colorado in the USA have had many benefits. They provide a regular supply of clean water to cities such as Las Vegas and the flow is regulated so there is a continuous flow. The dams also generate electricity, which is used by local homes, farms and factories.

Disadvantages of the schemes include the loss of land – flooded by reservoirs / lakes created behind the dams. Also, less sediment flows down the river which has led to smaller sandbanks so some animals have lost their habitats and some native species of fish have been affected too. Another negative is that sediment builds up behind the dams and has to be removed from time to time to keep the hydroelectric power generators working.

Now try this

1 Which of the following is **not** an example of a water management scheme? **(1 mark)**

☐ **A** dam ☐ **C** aquifer
☐ **B** reservoir ☐ **D** water harvesting

2 Explain **two** reasons why large-scale water management schemes are built. **(4 marks)**

Large-scale water management 2

You also need to know an example of a large-scale water management scheme in the developing world.

The Three Gorges Dam, China

Benefits

👍 The flood risk for homes, farms and factories along the Yangtze river is reduced.

👍 Water for **irrigation** is available from the lake which formed behind the dam.

👍 **Hydroelectric power** (HEP) is generated by the turbines in the dam. It is the world's largest capacity HEP station.

👍 The hydroelectricity means that China produces far less greenhouse gases from burning coal and oil (the project saves 31 million tonnes of coal each year).

👍 The river is more **navigable** for ships and so transport has improved.

Disadvantages

👎 Good farmland has been lost because of the lake.

👎 Over 1.3 million people were forced to move their homes.

👎 Important cultural and archaeological sites were lost.

👎 There is an increased risk of **landslides** in some places.

👎 The project was very expensive ($US 22.5 billion).

👎 **Sediment** is building up behind the dam.

👎 Downstream areas may become more liable to flooding because sediment flow in the river has been reduced so there is no sediment to maintain river banks.

👎 Important wetland areas have been destroyed.

Three Gorges Dam

The student has written three benefits, but one of these is wasted – only **two** separate reasons are needed to get the marks.

Worked example

State **two** ways in which a large-scale water management project has **benefitted** the area.

(2 marks)

Example: The Three Gorges Dam project in China

1 It has reduced flooding along the Yangtze river.

2 It generates hydroelectricity for homes and businesses.

3 It also provides water for irrigation.

Now try this

1 Explain the main ways in which a large-scale water management project has created **problems** in the local area. **(6 marks)**

2 Explain why the downstream areas of a large dam such as the Three Gorges Dam may become more liable to flooding. **(4 marks)**

Small-scale water management

In the developing world there are many small-scale, intermediate technology solutions to unreliable water supplies. You need to know at least one named example of this.

Wells, pumps and water barrels are examples of **intermediate technology** or **small-scale** water management systems.

Small-scale

These schemes are relatively cheap to build and maintain, cover small / very small areas are organised at a local level by local people, charities, local organisations, etc. and usually help local people access clean water and increase water storage.

Wells

Wells are dug to reach underground water. They are lined with concrete and have a concrete lid to prevent pollution by sewage.

Hand pumps

A hand pump is a more efficient way of reaching underground water. There is less chance of the water becoming **contaminated**.

Water barrels collect rainwater from gutters and can be stored and used in times of drought. This is called **water harvesting**. The water stays clean in the covered barrel.

Rain barrel

Using local media to improve water quality and use

A local radio soap in Tanzania, called *Pilika Pilika* (Busy Busy), includes messages about the importance of basic **hygiene** such as washing regularly and **sanitation**, and not polluting **drinking water** supplies with sewage. In one episode, a character fell into a well that had been polluted by toilet water, an unpleasant experience!

Worked example

Choose **one** water improvement project based on intermediate technology and explain some of the **costs** and **benefits** of the project. **(4 marks)**

Over 70% of Tanzania's rural population and 30% of its urban population do not have access to safe water. WaterAid is an agency that has helped communities to construct new wells and to use intermediate technology. The technology is a hand pump to raise water which is called the Afridev pump. The benefits are that the pumps are cheap to install, easy to use and because the pump can easily be repaired by the villagers they don't have to wait for outside help which could take days in rural communities. Although there are better pumps which could raise more water more quickly and break down less often, these need specialist engineers to repair them when they break down.

Now try this

Remember, the question asks about both the **amount** of water supplies and their **quality**, so make sure you cover both.

1 Using examples, explain how intermediate technology water management can affect the **volume** and **quality** of water supplies. **(4 marks)**

2 Explain how **two** methods using intermediate technology can improve water supplies for local people. **(4 marks)**

Coastal landforms and erosion

You need to be able to identify coastal landforms and understand how they have been created.

How waves erode the coast

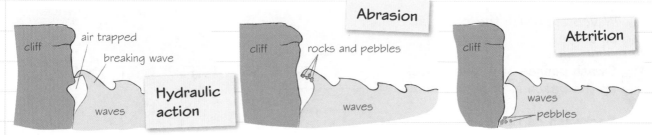

Waves hitting the rock forces pockets of air into cracks. Trapped air, released quickly, breaks up the rock.

Waves pick up stones and hurl them against the cliff which wears away the rock.

Pebbles carried by waves become rounder and smaller as they collide with each other.

Hard rock coastal landforms created by erosion

Caves, arches and stacks

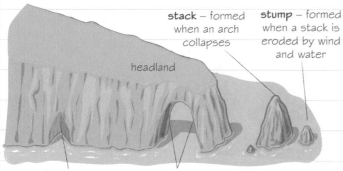

stack – formed when an arch collapses

stump – formed when a stack is eroded by wind and water

headland

cave – formed when the waves erode a weakness in the rock such as joint or a fault

arch – formed when two caves erode back from either side of a headland and meet in the middle

Wave-cut platforms

The erosion of cliffs can create wave-cut platforms – areas of flat rock at the base of the cliff.

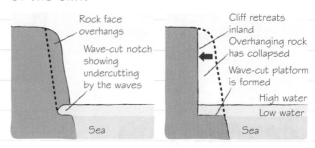

Rock face overhangs

Wave-cut notch showing undercutting by the waves

Sea

Cliff retreats inland
Overhanging rock has collapsed

Wave-cut platform is formed

High water
Low water

Sea

Worked example

Which **one** of the following statements is correct? **(1 mark)**

Destructive waves erode the coast (take material away) because they:

☐ **A** have a strong swash and weak backwash.

☐ **B** are small and weak with a low frequency.

☑ **C** have a weak swash and strong backwash.

☐ **D** have a long wavelength.

Now try this

1 State **three** ways in which waves erode a coast.

(3 marks)

2 Use diagram(s) to explain how a wave-cut platform is formed.

(4 marks)

Coastal landforms and deposition

Constructive waves have a long wavelength, a strong swash and a weak backwash which means they deposit material at the coastline forming various features you need to know.

Longshore drift

1 Waves approach the coast at an angle.

2 **Swash** pushes sand and gravel up the beach at the same angle.

3 **Backwash** carries sand and gravel back down the beach at 90° under the force of gravity.

4 Sand and gravel move along the beach in a zigzag fashion.

5 Sand is lighter than gravel so moves further up the beach.

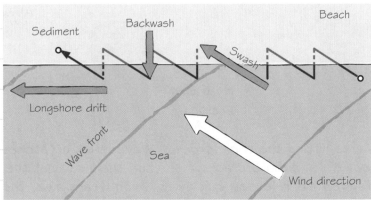

Adapted diagram courtesy of Barcelona Field Studies Centre, www.geographyfieldwork.com

Formation of sand spits

When there is a bend in the coastline, **longshore drift** carries the sand beyond the bend. It builds up as a **sand spit**.

If longshore drift continues along the spit, it may join up with the coastline on the other side, of for example a bay, to form a **bar**.

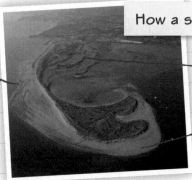

How a sand spit is formed

Behind the spit, the sheltered water becomes a **salt marsh**.

The end of the spit is curved where it meets strong winds and waves.

Worked example

1 Explain how a **bar** is formed. **(4 marks)**

Sand and pebbles are moved along the coast by longshore drift. Where the coastline changes direction, sand and pebbles are deposited and this starts to build up until a spit is formed. Over time, the sand and pebble accumulation grows larger and builds across an estuary to form a bar. The bar cuts off rivers from the sea so water builds up behind the bar to form a freshwater lake or lagoon such as at Slapton Ley in Devon.

2 Describe the process of how longshore drift operates. **(4 marks)**

When waves approach the coast at an angle, they break. The swash pushes sand and gravel up the beach at the same angle. The backwash drags the sand and gravel back down the beach at a 90° angle due to gravity. This gives a zigzag movement of material along the beach and this repeated process is called longshore drift. The smallest material is sand and this is moved easily so ends up at the top of the beach. The pebbles are heavier and are not moved as far.

Now try this

1 Briefly describe how spits are formed. **(2 marks)**

2 Describe the features of a constructive wave. **(2 marks)**

Geology of coasts

Soft rock coasts

Soft rocks such as clay are easily eroded by the sea. An example of a soft rock coast is Holderness in Yorkshire. Cliffs at a soft rock coast:

- may be high but less rugged and less steep than hard rock coasts
- will have piles of mud and clay on the face and at the bottom of the cliff
- will have very few hard rocks at the foot of the cliff.

Hard rock coasts

Hard rocks such as granite are resistant to erosion. An example of a hard rock coast is Land's End in Cornwall. Cliffs at a hard rock coast:

- will be high, steep and rugged
- will have a bare cliff face
- will have some rocks and boulders at the foot of the cliff
- will have erosion features such as caves, arches and stacks.

Formation of Lulworth Cove

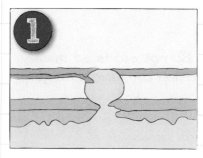 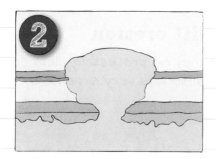 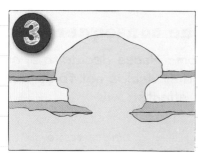

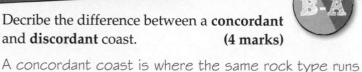
☐ Chalk ■ Greensand ☐ Wealden clay ■ Purbeck beds ☐ Portland limestone ■ River

Waves slowly cut through a weakness in the resistant band of **limestone** (and Purbeck beds) caused by a river cutting a valley through the limestone. This formed the small entrance to the cove.

Waves erode the soft band of **clay** quite quickly.

The band of chalk behind the clay band is more resistant so is slowing the rate of erosion inwards, although erosion is occurring sideways, forming the cove shape.

Worked example

HIGHER B–A

Decribe the difference between a **concordant** and **discordant** coast. **(4 marks)**

A concordant coast is where the same rock type runs along the coastline. A discordant coast is where the rock type alternates in bands along the coastline, which produces a different set of coastal features.

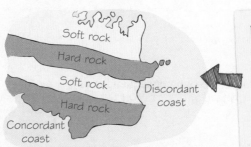

Properly labelled diagrams to illustrate your answers will gain you marks, so don't be afraid to use them!

Now try this

1 Identify **two** landforms found along a discordant coast. **(2 marks)**

 FOUNDN D–C

2 Using named examples, explain the main differences between soft rock coasts and hard rock coasts.

(8 marks + 3 marks SPaG)

 HIGHER A–A*

Check that your spelling, punctuation and grammar are really good and that your answer is clear.

Factors affecting coastlines

Rock type – hard rocks erode more slowly than soft rocks.

 1

Number of joints and faults – rocks with more faults and joints erode more quickly than rocks with fewer joints and faults.

 2

Fetch – if the wind blows over a wide area of sea (**fetch**), the waves are stronger and will have a greater impact on the cliffs.

3

> How fast a coast retreats depends on...

Cliff exposure – cliffs exposed to strong winds and weather will erode more quickly than sheltered cliffs.

 4

Storms – cliffs exposed to frequent storms will erode more quickly.

 5

Sea defences – some cliffs are protected by sea defences which will slow retreat down.

6

The consequences of cliff erosion

Some places decide to spend money on protecting cliffs so they do not erode so quickly. If they decide not to do this because it is very expensive, cliff erosion can have a range of effects.

Houses destroyed

Farmland lost

Loss of income

Hotels and caravan parks abandoned

Loss of roads

Worked example

 D-C

Explain how climate change may affect coasts in the future. **(4 marks)**

Sea levels are predicted to rise because of climate change. This will mean that low-lying coastal areas, such as in Bangladesh, are at risk of flooding. Some islands, for example the Maldives, might completely disappear into the sea.

It is likely that there will be more frequent and stronger storms in some parts of the world. This will mean that coastlines are eroded faster and there may be more instances of coastal flooding which may damage people's properties and destroy depositional features such as beaches.

Now try this

 HIGHER C

1 State **two** possible impacts of climate change on coastal depositional features. **(2 marks)**

2 Describe **two** consequences of cliff erosion. **(4 marks)**

 FOUNDN D-C

Coastal management

Coasts can be managed in different ways to defend them against the sea.

Hard engineering

Sea wall

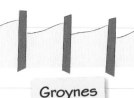

Groynes

Rip rap

Off-shore reef

👍 Protects cliffs and buildings

👎 Expensive

👍 Prevents sea removing sand

👎 Exposes other areas of coastline

👍 Rocks absorb wave energy

👎 Expensive

👍 Waves break on reef and lose power

👎 Expensive and may interfere with fishing

Holistic management and soft engineering

Beach replenishment

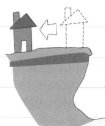

Managed retreat

Cliff regrading

👍 Sand reduces wave energy and maintains tourism

👎 Expensive

👍 People and activities avoid erosion by moving inland

👎 Expensive

👍 Reduces slippage

👎 Foot of cliff still needs protection from the waves

Worked example

Using a named example, explain the **costs** and **benefits** of hard engineering when managing a coastline   **(6 marks + 3 marks SPaG)**

In Swanage Bay, several hard engineering methods have been tried. In the 1920s, a sea wall was built to try and stop cliff erosion. The benefit is that it has succeeded in stopping the cliffs being eroded and has protected buildings close to the cliffs. However, the sea wall was very expensive to build and is expensive to maintain. Another method that has successfully stopped cliff erosion is rock armour which has been placed at the foot of the cliff in some areas.

Groynes on the beach aim to reduce longshore drift. Their benefit is that they stop the beach from disappearing, which helps tourism as well as protecting the coastline from sea erosion. These methods are expensive but some people also say they spoil the look of the coastline.

Now try this

1 Outline the main advantages and disadvantages of hard engineering methods to protect coasts.   **(8 marks + 3 marks SPaG)**

2 State **two** examples of soft engineering to manage coasts.   **(2 marks)**

Rapid coastal retreat

You need to know a case study of coastal retreat and the threats this poses to people and the environment. You also need to know some conflicting views on how this should be managed.

Holderness coast

- 60 km of coastline in East Yorkshire.
- Low cliffs of soft boulder clay with narrow beaches. Easily eroded and prone to slumping when saturated.
- Cliff line is retreating at nearly 2 m every year.
- Most erosion during storms and tidal surges.
- Dozens of villages have been washed away; property prices have slumped.
- Management strategies: groynes and rock armour in Mappleton (£2 million) have been successful. Some areas are undefended.

Robin Hood's Bay
---- Coastline in Roman times
• Lost village or town
Scarborough
Flanborough Head
NORTH SEA
Position of cliff now
Mappleton
Hull
River Humber
Spurn Head
N
0   50 km

Map of Holderness

When questions ask for opinions of people, remember not to generalise in your answer. Everyone has different opinions so, for example, don't say that all residents want more hard engineering defences as not all will want that.

Worked example

For a named example of a coastline experiencing rapid coastal retreat, outline the conflicting views on how this should be managed.   **(8 marks + 3 marks SPaG)**

HIGHER
A - A*

The Holderness coast in Yorkshire is experiencing the fastest cliff retreat in Europe at nearly 2 m every year. There are many conflicting views about how to manage it. Some people, particularly politicians / councillors and some locals, think that the only option is to do nothing. This may be because of the expense involved and because of the small number of people affected. It may also be because of the possible environmental impacts of engineering to protect the coastline. Other local inhabitants believe that the existing defences should be maintained or even advanced using the current methods of hard engineering. They point out the cost of the loss of farmland, businesses, roads and homes if nothing is done. However, some people who live further along the coast believe that the existing hard engineering has caused more erosion further up and down the coast so they would disagree that any more needs to be done. Another option that some people want is called strategic realignment – this involves moving the defence line back and allowing some caravan parks, for example, to move further inland. This would be cheaper than building more hard engineering structures and would therefore be more sustainable, but home owners generally do not agree with it as it would not benefit them.

Now try this

For a named example of a coastline experiencing rapid coastal retreat, outline reasons for and against coastal management.   **(6 marks + 3 marks SPaG)**

FOUNDN
C

30

River systems

The key characteristics of a river change as it moves from its upper course, to its middle and lower courses.

Characteristics of stages of the course of the Afon Nant Peris

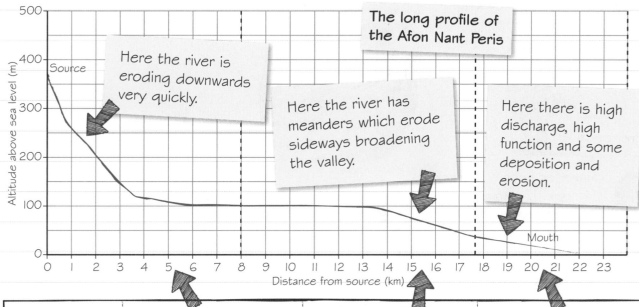

Here the river is eroding downwards very quickly.

The long profile of the Afon Nant Peris

Here the river has meanders which erode sideways broadening the valley.

Here there is high discharge, high function and some deposition and erosion.

Source

Mouth

Altitude above sea level (m)

Distance from source (km)

	Upper course	Middle course	Lower course
Gradient	steep	less steep	shallow gradient
Discharge	small	large	very large
Depth	shallow	deeper	deep
Channel shape	narrow, steep sides	flat, steep sides	flat floor, gently sloping sides
Velocity	quite fast	fast	very fast
Valley shape	steep sides	flat with steep sides	flat with gently sloping sides
Features	waterfalls, interlocking spurs.	meanders, floodplain.	meanders, floodplain, levees, ox-bow lakes.

Worked example

Which **one** of the following is the correct description of how a river changes from source to mouth? **(1 mark)**

☐ **A** It gets steeper and narrower as it moves towards the sea.

☑ **B** It gets flatter and wider as it moves towards the sea.

☐ **C** It gets steeper and wider as it moves towards the sea.

☐ **D** It gets flatter and narrower as it moves towards the sea.

Now try this

1 Describe the changes in **gradient** and **discharge** along the course of a river. **(4 marks)**

2 Describe the changes in **depth** and **channel shape** along the course of a river. **(3 marks)**

Start by underlining the most important words in the question.

Processes shaping rivers

Weathering and mass movement are the main processes that shape river valleys.

Weathering

The main forms of weathering which affect river valleys are:

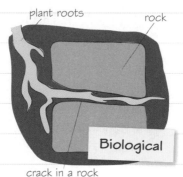

water accumulates in a crack in the rock, freezes and expands

rock

Freeze-thaw

plant roots   rock

Biological

crack in a rock

natural rainfall (slightly acidic)

rock

Chemical

weak point in the rock

1 Rainwater enters a crack in a rock. If it freezes, this exerts pressure on the rock and can eventually break it into smaller pieces.

2 Tree roots can penetrate cracks in rocks and split them apart.

3 Rainwater is slightly acidic and can dissolve some rocks, especially limestone and chalk.

Mass movement

The main forms of mass movement that affect river valleys are:

Soil creep

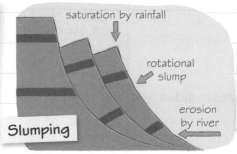

saturation by rainfall

rotational slump

erosion by river

Slumping

Rivers flowing over resistant rock tend to have steep sides. Rivers flowing over less resistant rock tend to have gentle slopes.

1 Particles of soil slowly move down the sides of valleys under the influence of gravity.

2 Valley sides are eroded by the river making the sides steeper and increasing the downward movement of material. Heavy rainfall can trigger this movement.

Worked example

Describe the processes of **weathering** that can occur on river valley sides. **(3 marks)**

Weathering is the breakdown of rocks and minerals by physical and chemical processes. One important process is freeze-thaw when rainwater enters a crack in a rock and in freezing, it expands and can crack the rock more. Similarly, tree roots can prise open cracks in rocks. Some rain is acidic and can dissolve rocks, including limestone and chalk.

Now try this

1 Describe how mass movement can affect valley sides. **(3 marks)**

2 Compare the ways in which freeze-thaw breaks up rocks with the ways biological weathering breaks up rocks. **(4 marks)**

Upper course landforms

In the upper course of a river, erosion is the main process at work, and creates various landforms.

Thornton Force waterfall in North Yorkshire

Mudstone
Where rivers flow over bands of rocks with different resistance, the softer rocks will be eroded more quickly. The River Twiss flows over limestone rocks then meets a band of mudstone. The mudstone wears away more quickly, creating a step which gradually becomes deeper. The step is now 10m high.

Overhang
Eventually the overhanging resistant rock will collapse, making the waterfall steeper. If this happens repeatedly, the position of the waterfall moves upstream. This is called **retreat**.

Undercutting
The water flows down over the resistant rock but when it reaches the less resistant rock underneath, it erodes it, cutting back into the rock and creating the overhang above.

Plunge pool
At the foot of the waterfall is a **plunge pool**. This is an area of deeper water that has been created by the rapid erosion of the mudstone as the waters plunge down. The higher the waterfall, the greater the speed of the water and the greater the rate of erosion.

Worked example

HIGHER **C**

Briefly describe how interlocking spurs form. **(2 marks)**

In the upper course of a river, near its source, the river has little power to erode rocks. Therefore, it flows around the harder, more resistant rock. This creates spurs that interlock on either side of the valley as the river moves downstream.

Now try this

1 Describe **one** type of river erosion.   **(2 marks)**

2 **Explain** how a plunge pool is formed.   **(3 marks)**

Look carefully at the command words for the questions.

Lower course landforms

When the river reaches the middle course, both erosion and deposition are at work but by the lower course, the main process acting on it is deposition.

Meanders

In a meander, the river swings from side to side. The force of the water swinging from side to side directs the fastest current and greatest force of water against the outside bank of the meander, forming a steep bank called a **river cliff**. On the inside edge of the meander, the current is slower and deposition of sand takes place, creating a gently sloping bank called a **slip-off slope**.

1 Plan view of a section of meander

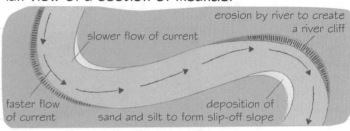

erosion by river to create a river cliff
slower flow of current
faster flow of current
deposition of sand and silt to form slip-off slope

2 Cross section through a meander

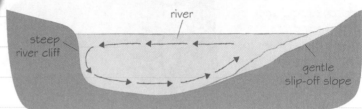

river
steep river cliff
gentle slip-off slope

The formation of an ox-bow lake

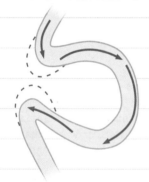  

1 Narrow neck of land is eroded.

2 Narrow neck of land is cut through and water takes quickest route. An ox-bow lake is formed.

3 Deposition seals off old meander and ox-bow lake begins to dry up.

Worked example

HIGHER B-A

The photograph shows a meander.

Describe the changes which may happen in this meander over a long period of time. **(4 marks)**

In time, the bends in the meander grow bigger until there is only a narrow neck of land between the bends. During a flood, the river may cut straight through this narrow neck forming a new channel. The old bend is abandoned, forming an ox-bow lake.

Now try this

1 Briefly describe the main process affecting the lower course of a river. **(2 marks)**

HIGHER C-B

2 Describe **two** features of a slip-off slope. **(2 marks)**

FOUND'N D-C

Causes and impact of flooding

You need to be able to interpret hydrographs, give physical and human causes of river flooding and explain its impact. You also need to investigate the impacts of flooding and the effectiveness of flood defences for a case study.

Hydrographs

In these hydrographs, the **lag time** – the time between the heaviest rainfall and the maximum level of the river – is very different.

- The Wye lag time is very short – the water runs over moorland which doesn't have much vegetation to absorb it.
- The Severn lag time is longer – the coniferous woodland absorbs the water and delays it in reaching the river.

The discharge of the Wye therefore reaches a higher amount, increasing the risk of flooding.

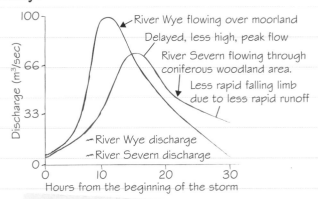

A hydrograph of the River Severn and Wye in July 2007

Worked example

HIGHER A-A*

Using a named example, describe the **impact** of river flooding. **(6 marks)**

The flooding of the rivers Ouse and Foss in November 2000 had many impacts on York. The water overcame the existing flood defences and flooded hundreds of homes and businesses in the centre of York. The army were called in to rescue people who were trapped in their homes and distribute sand bags and try to divert the water. Railway lines and roads were flooded so people and goods couldn't be transported. It cost York Council over £1 million to deal with the floods at the time. Longer term impacts were that house prices were reduced and people found it very expensive to get insurance for their homes and businesses. It prompted more flood defences to be built.

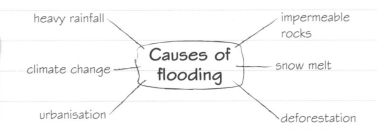

York floods, November 2000

Impacts

- homes and businesses flooded
- people evacuated, Army called in
- road and rail links cut off
- huge costs. Cost over £1 million to deal with and millions in insurance pay outs.

Existing defences

- flood warning systems
- sand bags for areas at risk
- raised embankments and flood walls.

These didn't prevent the floods in 2000, but they did reduce the impact and there were no fatalities. These floods prompted the government and council to improve defences further.

Now try this

Using a named example(s), explain the main **causes** of river flooding in an area you have studied.

(6 marks + 3 marks SPaG)

Remember to read the question carefully – it asks you to give **causes** of river flooding.

Managing river floods

Hard engineering methods

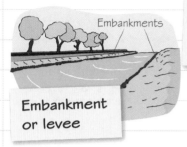

Embankments

Embankment or levee

Deepening and / or straightening the channel

Dam built upstream

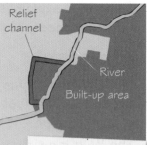

Relief channel

River

Built-up area

Relief channel

👍 Stops flood water from spreading

👎 Expensive

👎 May burst or water may go over

👍 Water flows away more quickly

👎 Defers flooding

👎 Unsightly

👍 Able to regulate and control flow of water

👎 Expensive

👎 Can burst

👍 Takes over flow water

👎 Expensive

👎 Disruptive and complex to build

Soft engineering methods

Washlands

Plant trees

(afforestation)

15m

5m

River

Pasture only

Pasture + crops

Road

Settlements and industry

Planning

Flood warning system

Severe flood warning in your area

👍 Cheap

👍 Water can go somewhere

👍 Can be used for special habitats

👍 The trees reduce the amount of water reaching the river

👍 Provides wildlife habitats

👎 Land cannot be used for anything else

👍 Building restricted to areas with low risk of flooding

👎 May cause planning problems elsewhere

👍 Prepares people

👎 Sometimes difficult to give enough warning

Worked example

HIGHER A–A*

Using named examples, examine hard **and** soft engineering approaches to managing river flooding. **(8 marks + 3 marks SPaG)**

York has had several hard engineering works to try to prevent and reduce the impact of the rivers Ouse and Foss flooding. Raised embankments made from earth and some from concrete and steel have been built around the rivers that flood. Upstream, the rivers' banks have been raised and sluice controls built to let water in and out of a natural floodplain. All of this has been extremely expensive and only partly successful as flooding has still occurred. In contrast, soft engineering methods have been used around the River Skerne in north-east England. Here, wetland habitats have been created alongside the river and industrial spoil has been removed to create a natural floodplain. In addition, the river's natural meanders have been restored so the water moves more slowly. This has been far …

Now try this

Explain some of the advantages and disadvantages of different **soft engineering** methods of river management.

FOUNDN C

(6 marks + 3 marks SPaG)

You would need to add other developed examples to do well.

Threats to the ocean

You need to know how either the global pattern of coral reefs or mangrove swamps have changed over the past 50 years and what the effects of this might be.

What is a marine ecosystem?

'Marine' means to do with the sea or ocean and 'ecosystem' describes the animals and plants that are linked to parts of the local physical environment. You will probably have studied either mangrove swamps or coral reefs, but whichever one you have studied, make sure you know where these ecosystems are located (distributed), what it is like and why and how it is valuable to humans.

What are mangrove swamps?

Swampy forest

A mangrove swamp

Adapted to daily flooding and salty conditions

Twisty roots which trap mud providing a great habitat for marine life

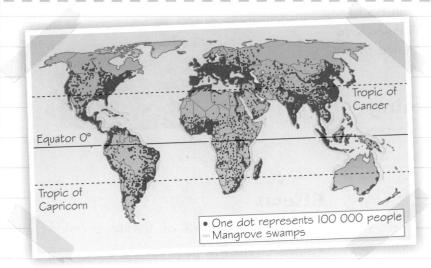

Equator 0°

Tropic of Cancer

Tropic of Capricorn

• One dot represents 100 000 people
— Mangrove swamps

1 Mangrove swamps are located along shorelines in **tropical** and **subtropical** zones.

2 They are often in highly populated areas such as central America, west Africa, and south Asia.

3 Over the past 50 years, around 50% of mangroves have been destroyed.

Impacts for humans

Loss of mangrove swamps will mean:

- less protection against tsunamis
- loss of shelter and breeding areas for fish so fishing will be affected
- fewer tourists visiting as habitats for marine and other wildlife will die
- local people not benefitting from big prawn farms.

Worked example

Using a named example, explain how climate change is threatening a marine ecosystem.   **(6 marks + 3 marks SPaG)**

Mangrove swamps are a marine ecosystem. They are found on coastlines in tropical and subtropical areas. But rising sea levels could drown the mangroves and they would die. Climate change could also mean that seawater becomes less salty everywhere, because of the polar ice caps melting (ice caps are made of fresh water). Mangroves and the fish that live in them are specially adapted to live in salty conditions so they might not be able to adapt and will die.

Now try this

D-C

Describe what is meant by the term 'marine ecosystem'.   **(2 marks)**

Ecosystem change

For **either** mangrove swamps **or** coral reefs, you need to know how human activities and climate change put this ecosystem under threat.

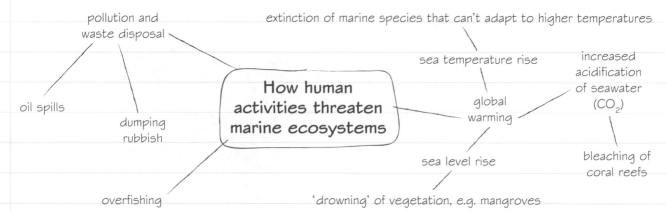

pollution and waste disposal

extinction of marine species that can't adapt to higher temperatures

sea temperature rise

increased acidification of seawater (CO_2)

oil spills

How human activities threaten marine ecosystems

global warming

dumping rubbish

sea level rise

bleaching of coral reefs

overfishing

'drowning' of vegetation, e.g. mangroves

Prawn farming

The long, twisting roots of mangrove swamps make an ideal habitat for prawns. These can be fished sustainably, however over half of all mangrove swamps have been cleared for intensive prawn farming (especially in Asia).

Commercial prawn farming

Mangrove swamp is cleared and large ponds are dug in the mud.
Prawns from the local area (and other parts of the world) are put into the ponds.
Antibiotics and pesticides are added to the ponds.
Millions of large prawns are harvested.
Waste water from ponds is dumped into the sea.

Effects

- creates problems of coastal erosion
- loss of habitat
- loss of defence against tsunami
- pollution from antibiotics and pesticides used in prawn farming.

Worked example

HIGHER C-B

Explain how **bleaching** may lead to a decline in the number of marine species. **(2 marks)**

Coral bleaching is where corals are discoloured as a result of being damaged. It happens either because of increasing temperatures, acidification or sediment in the water. Species that feed on the coral will decline because they will have less to feed on.

Now try this

Using a named example, **examine** why marine ecosystems should be managed for the future. **(8 marks + 3 marks SPaG)**

HIGHER A-A*

Pressure on the ecosystem

Unsustainable use of marine ecosystems can disrupt food webs and nutrient cycles, which threatens the extinction of some plants and animals. You need to know about the physical processes that disrupt food webs.

A marine food web

Energy is lost at each step up the chain. There are more organisms at the bottom of the web than at the top.

Food webs are highly interconnected: a change in one part quickly causes changes in other parts.

A food web illustrates the relationship between plants and animals in an ecosystem.

A food web also balances the nutrients in an ecosystem. Nutrients, such as nitrogen, are used and re-used by different organisms in the food web – this is called the nutrient cycle.

Top predators, such as the shark, use a lot of energy chasing prey and need a lot of prey to survive.

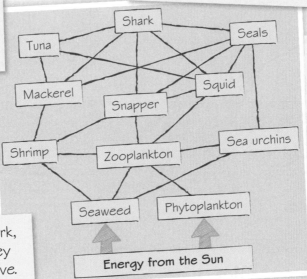

How the food web can be disrupted

1 **Overfishing** is when one species is fished more than is sustainable. For example, overfishing of tuna can decrease shark numbers but increase mackerel. Some species have been fished to extinction, e.g. Baiji white dolphin.

2 **Eutrophication** is the run-off of, for example, nitrate fertilisers from the land into the sea which causes overfeeding and algal bloom. This uses up the oxygen in the water and species suffocate.

3 **Siltation** is when plants near the coast get buried in silt from soil which has been washed into the sea. These plants can't reach the sunlight and they die.

Worked example

FOUND'N E-D

Study the food web above.

Which **one** of the following would result from a decline in the population of phytoplankton? **(1 mark)**

☐ **A** An increase in seaweed.
☑ **B** A decrease in all other species.
☐ **C** A decrease in zooplankton.
☐ **D** An increase in all other species.

Now try this

1 Describe the impact of a decline in phytoplankton on the shark population in the marine food web above. **(2 marks)**

If a question asks you to refer to a source make sure you use it.

2 Outline **one** of the main processes that can disrupt marine food webs. **(2 marks)**

Localised pressures

You need to know a case study of a local-scale marine ecosystem that is under pressure and show how local groups may disagree on how it should be managed.

Pressure in the Firth of Clyde

Overfishing
Firth of Clyde completely overfished, e.g. Lamlash Bay overfished for scallops

Sewage disposal
Tougher laws have stopped disposal of sewage from homes straight into the sea

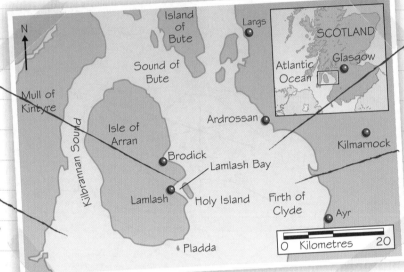

Tourism
Yachting, kayaking, diving are popular activities along the coastline but they disturb wildlife

Military testing
Firth of Clyde is used as nuclear submarine testing ground

Firth of Clyde conflict

Government 'no-take' zone policy	Increase tourism	Oil and gas exploration
👍 Increased fish, seals and porpoises, also good for tourism.	👍 Boosts local economy.	👍 Provides jobs.
👎 Fishermen have lost jobs.	👎 Disrupts wildlife.	👎 Increases pollution and spoils landscape.

Worked example

Using an example(s), explain why local groups sometimes have conflicting views on the management of a marine ecosystem. **(8 marks + 3 marks SPaG)**

The Firth of Clyde in Scotland has been overfished for many years, particularly in Lamlash Bay where heavy dredging machinery has killed off whole areas of the seabed. The Scottish Government has made the area a no-take zone, which means no fishing is allowed. Local fishermen are very upset about this. They would prefer better management of fishing techniques. But tourism firms like the ban because they can earn money taking tourists to see seals and porpoises. The main disagreement is therefore about how local people can make a living from this ecosystem...

EXAM ALERT!

In questions like this, be sure to give some **different** views and then explain why those different views are held.

Students have struggled with exam questions similar to this – **be prepared!** ResultsPlus

Now try this

Explain why human population increase may put a greater pressure on coastal marine ecosystems.

(2 marks)

Local sustainable management

You need to know two local case studies of marine management. Sustainable management is needed at the local scale if the oceans are going to be protected. It...

☑ makes sure an environment recovers quickly from any use

☑ prevents damage to the environment

☑ helps local people benefit from their environment

☑ helps local people understand why this management benefits them.

Coral Triangle

Ecosystem: coral reef.

Location: South Pacific.

Threats:
- acidified seawater
- growing population pressure leading to overfishing
- pollution
- run-off.

Management plan (joint government partnership):
- marine protection areas
- sustainable fishing rules
- protection of threatened species
- planning for climate change.

What makes it sustainable?:
- protects ecosystem from damage
- allows overfished species to recover
- involves local people.

Issues: it is difficult to enforce rules because of size of area.

Shetland Islands

Ecosystem: coastal.

Location: North Sea.

Threats: overfishing by technology-assisted commercial fishing (factory ships, sonar, etc.).

Management plan (Shetland Aquaculture):
- fish farms where fish are kept in caged enclosures away from rest of ecosystem
- wide range of fish farmed
- employs 1200 people.

What makes it sustainable?:
- takes commercial fishing pressure off marine ecosystem
- involves local people.

Issues:
- fish diseases spread quickly
- farmed fish escape and go back to marine ecosystem.

With the case study you have looked at, make sure you know:
- the problems and pressures on the ecosystem
- the management plan
- what makes the plan sustainable.

Worked example

Outline **one** reason why commercial fishing is sometimes viewed as being unsustainable. **(2 marks)**

Commercial fishing aims to catch as many fish from a target species as possible. This can overfish the species and it cannot recover its numbers in the near future.

Now try this

1 Compare **two** approaches to sustainable management of marine resources. **(4 marks)**

2 Comparing **two** approaches to sustainable management, outline which **one** gives most benefit to local people. **(2 marks)**

Global sustainable management

The pressure people put on marine ecosystems is rising in part because of increased demand for resources. You need to know about global-scale actions to protect ocean ecosystems.

Protecting whales

Global agreements to protect whales

👍 The International Whaling Convention (IWC) bans commercial whale hunting.

👍 The 156 countries who signed the United Nations Convention on the Law of the Sea (UNCLOS) have to follow the IWC.

👍 Part of the Convention on International Trade in Endangered Species (CITES) provides local protection to all great whales.

Issues around protecting whales

👎 Japan defies international whaling laws.

👎 Norway objects to plans to make south Pacific a whale sanctuary.

👎 In the Faroe Islands, killing pilot whales is a culturally important event.

👎 Iceland hunts whales commercially and for scientific research.

International law

Protecting whales is a good example of how difficult it is to make international laws work:

- 60% of the ocean doesn't belong to any country and everyone wants a share
- not all countries agree or follow laws
- there are many different interest groups that the laws need to take account of
- it is very hard to enforce laws.

old tankers being phased out

using seawater to flush out oil tankers is banned

oil spills less likely

good

reduces pollution

Global pollution at sea

not so good

no one country will take responsibility to clear up

Pacific Garbage Patches (large areas of sea full of floating rubbish)

Worked example

E-D FOUND'N

Using an example, outline **one** international agreement that is attempting to create sustainable marine ecosystems.   **(2 marks)**

The International Whaling Convention bans all commercial whale hunting. This protects whale species from being overfished.

Now try this

C-B HIGHER

1   Explain **one** reason why global agreements designed to protect whales are not always successful.
    (2 marks)

C FOUND'N

2   Using examples, explain how international agreements are trying to protect marine ecosystems.
    (6 marks + 3 marks SPaG)

Make sure that your spelling, punctuation and grammar are really good.

Extreme climates: characteristics

The polar regions and hot arid areas are known as extreme environments because of their special characteristics. You need to be able to describe the climate of **both** polar and hot arid environments.

Polar regions are located in areas of high **latitude**. In contrast, hot arid areas cover more latitudes but most are located in the **tropics**.

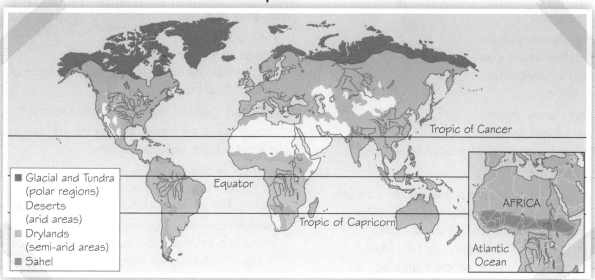

Tropic of Cancer

Equator

AFRICA

Tropic of Capricorn

Atlantic Ocean

■ Glacial and Tundra (polar regions)
  Deserts (arid areas)
■ Drylands (semi-arid areas)
■ Sahel

cold because of the high latitudes, the further north the more extreme the cold

winters are very cold (down to −50°C) with few or no hours of light

cold night temperature because there are very few clouds to keep heat in

occasional intense downfalls of rain that cause **flash flooding**

dry with less than 300 mm of **precipitation** per year falling mostly as snow

Polar climate

Hot arid climate

hot day time temperatures, often above 30°C

summers are short with many hours of light; this is the growing season in the **tundra**

there is very little seasonal change in very arid areas – slightly more in semi-arid areas

dry with sometimes less than 250 mm precipitation per year

the hottest arid environments support little plant, animal and human life

the coldest glacial regions support no life at all

Worked example

Which **one** of the following statements best describes the location of polar environments? **(1 mark)**

☐ A Near the Equator.
☑ B In high latitudes.
☐ C In low latitudes.
☐ D At various latitudes.

Variation

There is a lot of variation within extreme environments.

Polar
- Glacial = ice-covered (e.g. Greenland).
- **Tundra** = frozen soil (e.g. Alaska).

Hot arid
- Deserts = less than 250 mm rain per year (e.g. Sahara).
- **Drylands** = 250–500 mm rain per year (e.g. Sahel).

Now try this

Explain all your points **clearly** and give examples.

1 Describe the main **physical** characteristics of **hot arid regions**. **(4 marks)**

2 Explain the main **physical** characteristics of **polar regions**. **(2 marks)**

Why are extreme climates fragile?

The extreme environments of polar and hot arid areas make them very fragile places. You need to know the reasons for this, and how plants and animals have **adapted** to live in them.

Polar flora and fauna

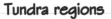

Glacial regions

- Support very little life other than some insects, arachnids and mice.
- Some hardy plants grow close to the ground to survive the strong winds.

Tundra regions

- Many animals, insects and birds can live in tundra regions. They are specially adapted to survive the cold with thick layers of fat and / or fur. Many are coloured white to camouflage themselves against the snow.
- Boggy conditions suit water-loving plants such as sedges and moss.

Hot arid flora and fauna

Semi-arid regions

- Animals store water in fat and tend to be nocturnal, spending the day underground out of the Sun.
- Insects collect moisture from the air.
- Some animals have, for example, large ears to help **dissipate** heat.
- Plants store water (acacia trees) and / or have extensive root systems to reach water far underground.
- Seeds can stay dormant for years and produce brightly coloured flowers to attract insects as soon as there is rainfall.

> Very arid regions have very little plant or animal life.

Extreme climates and climate change

Extreme climates are very vulnerable to climate change as their ecosystems are so fragile.

In **polar environments**, climate change can lead to:

- 👎 burst lakes – in glacial regions, where there is a build-up of melt water, lakes can burst their banks resulting in flood water destroying ecosystems
- 👎 **solifluction** – in tundra regions, large areas of soil melt and move like a landslide, destroying vegetation in its path.

In **hot arid environments**, climate change can lead to:

- 👎 extreme drought which even the specially adapted flora and fauna can't survive
- 👎 desertification where the area of desert increases – animals and plants that live in what used to be semi-arid areas cannot adapt and they die.

Worked example C-B

Explain **one** adaptation to the extreme conditions for an animal living in polar environments.   **(2 marks)**

Snowshoe hares live in Alaska. Their fur goes white in winter so they are camouflaged against the snow which helps protect them from predators.

Now try this

1 Describe **one** reason why extreme environments are described as **fragile**.   **(2 marks)**

2 Examine why **both** polar and hot arid regions are described as fragile environments.   **(8 marks + 3 marks SPaG)**

> Make sure you use your geographical terminology accurately and check that your spelling, punctuation and grammar are really good.

People and extreme climates

People can adapt to the challenges of extreme climates. You need to know about the adaptations people have made to living in both extreme polar and hot arid climates. You also need to know about the special cultures of some of the people living in these areas.

Polar environment – human adaptations

Hot arid environment – human adaptations

1 Adaptations to the cold:
- Triple glazing in houses.
- Wearing fur, wool, layers etc. to keep warm.
- Use of **geothermal power**.

2 Adaptations to frozen ground:
- Houses raised up above ground.
- Hunting rather than growing crops.
- Roads built on gravel to prevent them cracking with **solifluction**.

3 Adaptations to snow:
- Steep roofs so snow falls off.

1 Adaptations to the heat:
- Walls on buildings painted white to reflect heat.
- Thick walls and small windows to keep heat out.
- Air conditioning in homes.
- Wearing loose-fitting clothes.
- Wearing head coverings.

2 Adaptations to the lack of water:
- Flat roofs on buildings to catch water.
- Irrigation used to grow crops.
- **Nomadic farming** so areas aren't overgrazed by herds.

Worked example

HIGHER
C-B

Describe **one** feature of a culture of people living in extreme climates that makes them special. **(2 marks)**

In the Sahel, the Dogon people of Mali have created a distinctive and unique musical culture. They play instruments which are not found anywhere else in the world.

Now try this

'Outline' means you need to give a few details or write down the most important points.

1 Describe **one** way in which technology makes life easier for people living in polar environments. **(2 marks)**

2 Outline how money and technology risk damaging local cultures in hot arid environments. **(4 marks)**

Threats to extreme climates

You need to know about the main threats to extreme environments and how climate change could have an impact on traditional economies in these areas.

Impact in Alaska (polar)	Threat	Impact in Sahel (hot arid)
Oil spills (e.g. Exxon Valdez) have caused environmental catastrophes in Alaska in the past.	Pollution	Air pollution from newly emerging economies and industrialised countries may increase drought.
Permafrost melting due to buildings heating up land, especially around big urban centres.	Land degradation	Desertification leads to disappearing vegetation and soil erosion. It is partly caused by overgrazing of livestock.
Loss of native languages and cultural traditions – influence of Western cultures is growing.	Cultural dilution	Traditional rituals performed to entertain tourists. Western cultures have a strong influence.
People, especially the young, are moving away due to lack of social and employment opportunities.	Out-migration	People, especially the young, are moving away due to lack of opportunities.

Effect of climate change on extreme climates

Worked example

B-A

Explain how climate change threatens the survival of hot arid settlements.   **(3 marks)**

In the Sahel, a hot arid region, climate change could mean less rain and less reliable rainfall. Less rain could turn dryland areas into desert, which might lead to ecosystem changes and increased soil erosion as vegetation is lost and people would have nowhere to graze livestock. Less rain might mean that conflicts could flare up over control of water resources. Many people might leave and move to the cities, putting city infrastructure under increased strain.

Now try this

1 What is meant by the term '**species migration**'?   **(2 marks)**

2 Outline **one** possible impact of climate change on some species in a polar environment.   **(2 marks)**

Extreme environments: sustainable management

Sustainable management is needed if extreme environments are going to survive. You should know about a range of local actions aimed at achieving a sustainable future.

Sustainable management

- ✓ makes sure an environment can recover quickly from any use
- ✓ prevents damage to the environment
- ✓ helps local people get benefit from their environment
- ✓ helps local people understand the benefits.

Sustainable management in hot arid regions

In poorer areas of hot arid regions, e.g. Tanzania in east Africa, water management is very challenging. Large-scale projects such as large dams are generally too expensive and do not always meet the needs of local people. The most sustainable solutions involve **intermediate technology**.

Intermediate technology

- Lining **wells** with concrete avoids sewage contamination.
- **Hand pumps** pump water up from deeper underground and the top of the well can be capped with a concrete cover to prevent contamination.

Water is safely stored in **rain barrels** for later use.

Sustainable management in polar regions

Use geothermal power where available (e.g. Iceland, Alaska).

Have conservation zones to protect Arctic fauna and flora.

Sustainable management

Promote ecotourism.

Promote native cultures.

Protect the environment from pollution.

Fish farming as sustainable alternative to commercial trawling.

Worked example

Describe **one** benefit of ecotourism to local people living in extreme environments. **(2 marks)**

Ecotourism may promote local cultures and bring in money to the economy. Tourists may watch traditional performances and may buy local traditional artworks.

EXAM ALERT!

Remember to focus on exactly what the question is asking – in this example don't be distracted into talking about anything other than the benefits of ecotourism.

Students have struggled with exam questions similar to this – **be prepared!**

Now try this

1 Which of the following is a way in which local actions could protect a community living in a polar environment? **(1 mark)**

☐ **A** Encourage immigration.

☐ **B** Use of geothermal power.

☐ **C** Encourage heavy industry.

☐ **D** International treaty to limit climate change.

2 Outline **one** way in which intermediate technology could help people living in hot arid environments. **(2 marks)**

Extreme environments: global management

You need to know about global actions to protect extreme climates from climate change.

Agreements on climate change

Some international actions affect both polar and hot arid extreme environments:

1997
Kyoto Protocol: Commitment to reduce greenhouse gas emissions by around 5% by 2012

Problems: Increases in emissions by the US (didn't sign up) and China wiped out all reductions made by other countries.

Problems: Only agreed to make plans. Many had hoped for a binding agreement that would ensure countries stuck to tough limits.

2010
Cancun Agreements: funds to help develop clean technology and help developing countries cut emissions

2009
Copenhagen Accord: 190 countries agreed to limit global warming

Problems: Only agreed to make plans, many had hoped for a binding agreement that would ensure countries stuck to tough limits.

2011
Durban Agreement: 190 countries (including US and China) agree to legally binding emission cutting targets

Problems: Doesn't come into force until 2020, when many fear it will be too late.

Agreements – polar regions

1961 Antarctic Treaty

- Restricts commercial development.

1998 Protocol Environmental Protection

- Extended Antarctic Treaty with rigorous protection.
- No new activities allowed in Antarctica unless very low impact.

Agreements – arid regions

UN Convention to Combat Desertification

- Since 1994 aimed to combat land degradation, reduce poverty and develop sustainable solutions.
- Promotes 'bottom-up' solutions: local people get funding and advice.
- 195 countries agreed to give money, share information and act together.

Worked example

Using named examples, explain how global actions are attempting to protect extreme environments. **(6 marks + 3 marks SPaG)**

Polar regions are very vulnerable to global warming. There have been different global agreements to limit global warming. Some have been voluntary for countries. Others, such as the Kyoto Protocol (1997) and Durban Agreement (2011), set targets backed up by law. But emissions of greenhouse gases by the big polluting countries have risen far faster than any reductions made by other countries. A better way forward is shown by the Antarctic Treaty (1961). This set extremely strict rules for how the Antarctic can be used, to preserve its unique environment. It has been very successful, with all countries doing what it says.

Now try this

Using named examples, explain how local and global actions are helping to ensure the survival of extreme environments. **(8 marks + 3 marks SPaG)**

World population growth

You need to know trends in global population growth and future projections. You also need to know how population changes as a country develops, as shown in the demographic transition model (DTM).

Growth of world population

- World population has grown from 1 billion in 1804 to about 7 billion in 2012. The main reason for this rise is the fall in the death rate (DR).

- More recently, there has been a fall in the birth rate (BR). This means that the rate of population growth is predicted to slow down, though nobody knows when zero population growth will be reached. Some have suggested the early 2020s but others think global population will reach 10 billion by 2100.

The five different stages of the demographic transition model

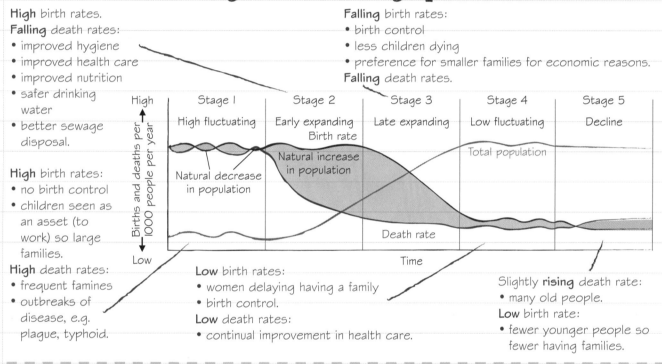

High birth rates.
Falling death rates:
- improved hygiene
- improved health care
- improved nutrition
- safer drinking water
- better sewage disposal.

High birth rates:
- no birth control
- children seen as an asset (to work) so large families.

High death rates:
- frequent famines
- outbreaks of disease, e.g. plague, typhoid.

Falling birth rates:
- birth control
- less children dying
- preference for smaller families for economic reasons.
Falling death rates.

Low birth rates:
- women delaying having a family
- birth control.
Low death rates:
- continual improvement in health care.

Slightly rising death rate:
- many old people.
Low birth rate:
- fewer younger people so fewer having families.

Worked example

Aim to develop your points, for example 'There are more doctors and nurses because ...'

Briefly describe why the **death rate** of the world's population has fallen in recent years. **(3 marks)**

The death rate has fallen because of better medicines and the introduction of immunisation schemes. There are also more doctors and nurses now, so medical attention is better. Houses are more hygienic with indoor toilets and there is better sewage disposal and safer drinking water. People also generally have a better diet.

Now try this

1 Outline some of the impacts of a falling birth rate. **(4 marks)**

2 State the **three** main features of Stage 1 of the demographic transition model. **(3 marks)**

Think about the birth and death rate as well as natural change.

Population and development

Countries at different stages of development will have different population structures, which can be shown by their population pyramids.

Population pyramids:

- Show the number or percentage of different age groups for each gender in the population.
- Can be used as a snapshot to show what stage of the DTM a country is at.
- Change shape as a country develops – the bottom narrow as the birth rate lowers; the top gets higher and wider as life expectancy increases.
- Show short-term factors that impact on population, e.g. war leading to a high death rate especially in young adult males.
- Can forecast population totals and growth rates to help future planning.

- Wide base = higher BR
- Narrow top = shorter life expectancy and fewer people surviving into middle age
- Youthful population

Indonesia 2011

- Narrow base = low BR
- Similar numbers in each age group = low DR
- Wide top = long life expectancy
- Ageing population

United Kingdom 2011

Worked example

Using examples you have studied, explain why **two** countries at different levels of development have different population structures. **(6 marks)**

The population of a developing country, such as Indonesia, has a shorter life expectancy than that of a developed country, such as the UK. This is because of the better living conditions, education and health care available in the UK, which means that more people are likely to live for longer. The population structure of the UK will therefore have a higher proportion of older people.

A developed country is also likely to have a smaller proportion of young people in its population structure because of a low birth rate. Small families are more likely because of better access to, and education about birth control. Better health provision also means that there is less need to have lots of children as they are more likely to survive.

Think about economic growth, demographic factors, migration and conflict.

Now try this

Study the UK's population pyramid. Identify which stage of the demographic transition model the UK is at. Give reasons for your answer. **(4 marks)**

Population issues

An ageing population is one where there is a high proportion of people aged over 65 years. A youthful population is one where there is a high proportion of people aged under 16 (or 18) years. Both of these situations cause different challenges that the government and people of a country have to deal with.

> Both ageing and youthful populations mean a country has a high number of dependants that the working population has to support both financially and socially. In both situations, the working-aged population may be unable, or choose not to work to look after either elderly relatives or children.

Ageing

More money needed for:

- state pensions
- social provision such as home help, meals on wheels, suitable housing
- medical provision, e.g. care homes, increased need for hospital beds and professionals to cope with diseases of the elderly, such as dementia.

Youthful

More money needed for:

- social provisions such as nurseries, schools, play grounds, child-specific benefits, e.g. maternity and paternity leave
- medical provisions, e.g. maternity units in hospitals, paediatric medical facilities, etc.

Worked example

HIGHER **B-A**

Explain some of the **problems** linked to youthful populations.   **(4 marks)**

Youthful populations mean there is a high proportion of young adults and children. This can be a problem because it puts a strain on the economically active people who have to support them either directly or through taxes, and sometimes they can't provide the services needed for the number of young dependents. For example, more schools and nurseries will need to be built and teachers and carers will be needed who may not be available.

Youthful populations also lead to population growth because of the continuing number of young adults who have children in the population – meaning a continued strain on resources such as housing.

Aim to fully explain at least two problems, and you could use examples to support your points.

Problems for the elderly in the UK

Difficulty of getting around if no public transport

Living alone when partners die

High cost of residential homes

Having to sell homes to pay for care

Long waits for hospital appointments and operations

Fear of crime

Now try this

HIGHER **D-C**

1 Describe some of the problems of an increasingly ageing population.   **(3 marks)**

2 What is meant by the term 'greying population'?   **(2 marks)**

Managing populations

A sustainable population is one that can be maintained without harming the environment or quality of life of the people. Many countries try to manage their populations to achieve the goal of sustainability.

Overpopulation

When a country has more people than can be supported by its resources it is **overpopulated**.

Underpopulation

When a country has more resources than people it is **underpopulated**.

	Problems of overpopulation	Problems of underpopulation
Resources	Not enough resources – may lead to malnutrition and starvation.	Not enough people to exploit the resources.
Services	Shortages of housing and educational and medical services.	Not enough people to pay taxes for services.
Employment	Unemployment – poverty for individuals and strain on benefits.	Underemployment / skills shortages negatively affect economy.
Other issues	Overcrowding leading to poor living conditions, especially in urban areas.	Often an ageing population – low fertility.

See also p. 51

For more on ageing populations.

How can populations be made sustainable?

👍 Making sure there are not too many and not too few people.

👍 Making sure there are enough people of working age to support the rest of the population.

👍 Managing resources so as not to use too many.

👍 Recycling resources as much as possible.

👍 Looking after the environment.

Worked example

D-C

Outline **two** examples of problems which may happen if a country's population is not sustainable. **(4 marks)**

If a country has fewer people than it needs, one of the problems might be that there are skills shortages in employment which will mean that the country's economy will suffer. If a country has more people than it needs, this will put a lot of pressure on resources such as food and housing and services, including hospitals and schools.

'Outline' means you need to give a few details or write down the most important points.

Now try this

Make sure you know the key geographical terms.

1 Explain what is meant by a **sustainable** level of population in a country. **(4 marks)**

B-A

2 What is meant by the terms:
(a) overpopulation
(b) underpopulation. **(2 marks)**

D-C

Pro- and anti-natal policies

One of the two ways in which governments try to manage population is through trying to increase or decrease the birth rate. You need to know an example of a country which has used pro-natalist policies and an example of a country which has used anti-natalist policies.

Anti-natalist policy: China

Why?
Huge rate of population growth led to a series of famines in the mid-20th century.

How does it work?
- Incentives given for having just one child: cash bonuses, longer maternity leave, better childcare, preferential access to housing.
- Young people persuaded to delay marriage.
- Pressure for abortion of 'unauthorised' pregnancies.
- Easy access to contraception and encouragement of post-pregnancy sterilisation.
- 'Forced' sterilisation of couples who have more than one child.

What is the policy?
One child policy. Encourages couples to have only one child and penalise those who have more.

Has it been successful?
Yes, the birth rate has fallen and so has the population growth rate. Less successful (and not as rigorously enforced) in rural areas. The policy has been relaxed a little in some regions since 1996.

What are the consequences?
- There haven't been any more huge famines.
- Widespread sex-selective abortion – more boys than girls being born which has led to shortage of women to marry and increase in bride kidnapping and prostitution.
- Possibly a future labour shortage and ageing population.

Pro-natalist policy: Singapore

Why?
Policy of reducing population growth from the 1960s was so successful it led to population decline and ageing population.

How does it work?
- Incentives for having more than two children include: tax rebates, cheap nurseries, preferential access to best schools, spacious apartments.
- Counselling offered to discourage abortions and sterilisation.
- Works alongside immigration policy that encourages young graduates (of child-bearing age) to immigrate to Singapore.

What is the policy?
'Have three or more – if you can afford it'. Offers incentives for couples to have lots of children especially those who are well-educated (and therefore higher earners).

Has it been successful?
Yes, the birth rate has increased and helped increase population.

Worked example

D-C

Give **two** examples of ways in which a government may try to increase the birth rate. **(2 marks)**

1 Provide good maternity pay and leave so women can afford time off work to have children and look after them when very young.
2 Provide cheaper access to good childcare (e.g. nurseries) for those having more children.

Now try this

G-E

1 Which of the following is correct? Pro-natalist policies:
   ☐ **A** encourage immigration.
   ☐ **B** encourage emigration.
   ☐ **C** encourage people to have fewer children.
   ☐ **D** encourage people to have more children. **(1 mark)**

2 Using a named example, examine how **one** country has tried to **reduce** the birth rate. **(6 marks)**

Had a look ☐ Nearly there ☐ Nailed it! ☐

Migration policies

Migration is the flow of people in and out of a country. Governments may try to manage their country's population through policies to promote or reduce immigration.

1 Open-door

Allows anyone to come to live in a country. Countries may run advertising campaigns abroad (usually aimed at certain groups) to encourage people to come and live in their country. There is an open-door policy for migration between EU countries.

2 Quotas

This **restricts** the number of people allowed into a country per year. Can be a total number allowed, a total number from a particular area or a particular type of person.

3 Skills tests

Potential migrants have to pass a 'skills test'. This ensures that only highly skilled and qualified migrants are allowed. It may also involve a points system where you have to have skills in certain areas to get enough points to qualify to be admitted.

Why encourage immigration?

- 👍 Can help address underpopulation.
- 👍 Helps address labour shortages – immigrants often do jobs the native population don't want to do.
- 👍 Meets specific skills shortages: doctors, teachers, engineers, etc.
- 👍 Working-aged immigrants pay taxes which help pay for services.
- 👍 Immigrants add to a country's culture and talent.

Tensions

- 👎 Pressures on housing, health care and education caused by immigrants.
- 👎 Fear by native population that immigrants are 'taking their jobs'.
- 👎 Discrimination / abuse of immigrants.
- 👎 Perception that immigrants take advantage of state benefits.
- 👎 Can alienate 'native' population.
- 👎 Quotas or skills tests may cause problems for people who want to bring family to live with them.

Worked example

HIGHER B-A

Outline why countries have different migration policies. **(4 marks)**

Countries have different policies for a number of reasons. If a country is overpopulated and there is a shortage of resources then it may probably have strict migration policies so few people are allowed into the country. For example, it could set immigration quotas so only a certain number of immigrants are allowed per year. However, if a country is underpopulated then it will have policies which encourage immigration such as an 'open-door' policy. If a country has a skills shortage or needs workers in a particular area then it might have a policy of skills tests or only allow people with the right skills or qualifications to migrate to the country.

Now try this

1 Describe how skills tests are used to limit the numbers of migrants allowed into a country.
(2 marks)

HIGHER C-B

2 Describe **one** policy which encourages immigration which may help an underpopulated country.
(2 marks)

FOUNDN E-D

Types of resources

Resources can be grouped into three main types: renewable, sustainable and non-renewable. You need to know the different types and be able to define and classify energy, mineral, physical and biological resources.

The three categories of resources

Non-renewable
Fixed amount available and can't be remade / renewed over a short period of time (e.g. coal).

Renewable
Resources that don't need to be managed to renew themselves (e.g. wind, sunlight).

Sustainable
Resources that can be managed so they renew themselves (e.g. wood).

 1 Energy
- Uses: heating, cooking, transport, electricity, etc.
- Examples: oil, coal, gas, water, sunlight
- Category: non-renewable and renewable

 3 Physical
- Uses: energy
- Examples: water, wind and sunlight
- Category: renewable

Types of resources

 2 Mineral
- Uses: building, jewellery making, manufacture
- Examples: iron ore, diamond, quartz, stone
- Category: non-renewable

 4 Biological
- Uses: food production, energy, manufacture
- Examples: biofuels, wheat, timber, fish
- Category: sustainable

Worked example

HIGHER B

Explain why using renewable resources is more sustainable than using non-renewable resources. **(2 marks)**

Watch out! Resources in this classification can be of two types, e.g. coal is both an energy resource and a mineral resource.

Sustainable resource use means that future generations will be able to use the resources too. Non-renewable resources, such as oil, gas or coal, will run out and not be around for future generations to use. Resources including sunlight, wind or geothermal energy renew themselves naturally, making them available for future generations, so they are more sustainable.

Now try this

 FOUNDN G-E

1 State **two** disadvantages of non-renewable resources. **(2 marks)**

2 Outline some advantages and disadvantages of using more solar energy in the UK. **(4 marks)**

 HIGHER B-A

Resource supply and use 1

The global supply and use of resources is unequal. You need to know about these inequalities and about likely future pressures on supply and consumption.

The regions which generally consume the most resources are Europe, the USA and Japan.

Africa, South America and parts of Asia consume the least resources.

Some of the richest regions have few natural resources, e.g. Japan.

Some of the poorest regions are resource rich, e.g. Sudan.

There is inequality within countries as well as between them, e.g. poor people in the USA and rich people in India.

The poorest 20% consume only 1.3% of all global resources.

The richest 20% of humans consume over 86% of all global resources.

Changing patterns of resource demand and consumption

Economic growth
In developing countries resource consumption per person is low.
Some economies are growing rapidly.
Increased demand for cars, air conditioning, housing and technology.

International relations
Increasing demand for non-renewable resources.
Countries preserving their own resources and not exporting to other countries.

e.g. Middle East supplies of oil.	Conflict between countries.	e.g. Russian supplies of gas.

Worked example

FOUNDN G-E

Which of the following continents has the **lowest** resource consumption per person? **(1 mark)**

☐ **A** Europe
☑ **B** Africa
☐ **C** North America
☐ **D** South America

Look at the number of marks in multiple-choice questions as this is likely to tell you the number of answers required.

Now try this

Start by underlining the most important words in the question.

1 Describe what may happen to global demand for oil over the next 30 years. **(2 marks)**

FOUNDN D-C

2 In the future it is likely that there will be more pressure on energy supplies. Explain the pressure that could result from global economic growth and changing international relations. **(4 marks)**

HIGHER B-A

Resource supply and use 2

You need to know the reasons for variation in supply and consumption of one non-renewable energy resource and one renewable energy resource.

Oil supply and consumption

Oil is found in many parts of the world and it is consumed by every country in the world.

As countries develop, their demand for oil is likely to increase.

More developed countries generally consume more oil than less developed countries.

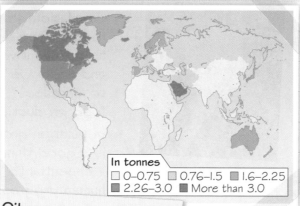

In tonnes
☐ 0–0.75 ☐ 0.76–1.5 ☐ 1.6–2.25
☐ 2.26–3.0 ☐ More than 3.0

Oil consumption in tonnes per head (2010)

There are big differences in oil consumption between different developed countries.

Governments and large companies pay for extraction, refining and transportation because they can make huge amounts of money selling it.

The USA has only 5% of the world's population but it uses 21% of the world's oil.

Hydropower supply and consumption

- 20% of the world's electricity is generated by hydroelectric power (HEP) – supplying one billion people.
- 99% of Norway's electricity comes from HEP.
- Generally more developed countries develop hydroelectric power stations. Nepal has huge potential for HEP but only a tiny fraction has been developed.

- 150 countries generate and use their own HEP. The largest are the USA, Canada, Brazil and China.
- Environmental factors can prevent development of suitable sites.
- Hydroelectric power can only be produced in situ, whilst oil can be transported to other places.

Worked example

FOUND'N
C-B

Explain the reasons for variations in the global supply and consumption of a **renewable** energy resource.   **(4 marks)**

Read the question carefully. This refers to a renewable resource, and make sure you refer to both supply and consumption.

Hydroelectric power is a renewable energy resource. It is available where there is flowing water and rain to maintain supplies. In countries which are flat or receive little rain, such as in parts of Africa, it would not be possible to generate hydroelectric power. Some places choose not to develop hydroelectric power because it would cause environmental damage, such as flooding large areas. Another reason why some countries, especially developing ones do not have hydroelectric power is that it costs a lot of money to build and maintain the necessary facilities.

Now try this

1 Describe what is meant by the idea of inequalities in resource supply and consumption.   **(2 marks)**

2 Identify **two** reasons for variations in the consumption of a non-renewable energy resource.   **(2 marks)**

Consumption theories

There are different theories about how well the world can cope with current resource consumption. You need to know about two of these theories and their differences.

Malthusian theory

Thomas Malthus

His theory:

- population growth went up geometrically: 2, 4, 8, 16, etc. (2 people have 4 children, those 4 children have 8 children between them, etc.)
- food production went up arithmetically: 1, 2, 3, 4 etc. – because improvements happen slowly
- this meant famines would occur to limit population size naturally
- the poor should realise that having lots of children was only making them poorer.

Contrary to Malthus' theory, food production has boomed due to new methods and technologies. However, some people have too much food and others have too little.

Boserupian theory

Her theory:

- population growth forces people to be inventive and find ways to increase food production
- population growth is a good thing – essential to human progress.

Ester Boserup

Boserup's theory didn't account for the fact that inventiveness can cause major environmental problems. In other words, we should be able to supply expanding populations with cars, fuel, meat and consumer goods but this has a big impact on the environment.

Worked example

Explain **one** advantage and **one** disadvantage to a country with rapid population growth. **(4 marks)**

HIGHER B

Advantage: population growth can be good for a country because it can lead to more effective use of resources and efficient farming methods.

Disadvantage: more people can mean more pollution, especially if resources are used wastefully, and pollution can make people's lives less pleasant and cause problems to the environment.

Now try this

1 Briefly describe the main differences between the theories of Malthus and Boserup. **(2 marks)**

2 Describe the difference between the terms 'resource supply' and 'resource consumption'. **(2 marks)**

Managing consumption

Local and national governments are trying to reduce resource consumption to try to achieve sustainability. You need to know how this can be done through education, conservation and recycling.

National and local governments

Education – changing behaviour	Conservation – maintaining health of natural world	Recycling
Advertising, schools, public awareness	Grants, quotas, programmes, laws, taxes	Recycling centres Door-to-door recycling collection Fines for companies who don't recycle
Reducing use of non-renewables and using them more efficiently: e.g. walking not driving, turning off lights, turning tap off when brushing teeth, etc.	For example, grants and subsidies for renewable energy, reducing car tax for less polluting cars, grants for solar panels and insulating homes, quotas on fishing, etc.	

National governments can pass laws and use tax money to educate its population and set up conservation projects in an attempt to become more sustainable.

Worked example

Describe how government policies can help reduce resource consumption. **(4 marks)**

Governments can make laws and fine businesses for producing lots of waste. They also fund education campaigns so people know about cutting their use of resources, such as the 'Switch it off' campaign. Another way is using money from taxes to give people grants to insulate their homes. They have also set up recycling schemes to encourage people to recycle rather than throw things out.

Sustainable development is development that meets the needs of the present without compromising the ability of future generations to meet their own needs.

(United Nations report, 1987)

EXAM ALERT!

Take care not to overwrite on this type of question. Try to make a few clear points or two developed points.

Students have struggled with exam questions similar to this – **be prepared!**

Now try this

Make sure you use relevant examples to support your points.

1 State **two** ways in which communities could waste less water overall. **(2 marks)**

2 Explain how national and local government policies can help to reduce resource consumption. **(6 marks)**

59

Potential of renewables

Another possible way to achieve sustainability is to develop alternative and renewable resources as well as technological 'fixes' to solve resource shortages.

Alternative and renewable resources

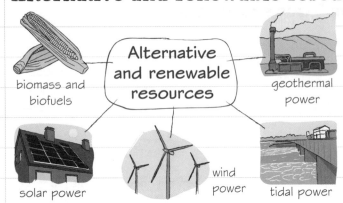

biomass and biofuels

Alternative and renewable resources

geothermal power

solar power

wind power

tidal power

Problems:

- renewables are generally not as efficient as non-renewables
- most renewables cannot meet the same demand as non-renewables
- not all countries have enough sun, wind, geothermal resources, area for biocrops, etc.
- the technology necessary to harness the energy from renewables is expensive.

Technological fixes

Boserup thought human inventiveness could solve the food problem – could it solve other resource problems?

Problem: Alternative to oil

Solution: Hydrogen fuel cells, e.g. to power cars

👍 There's lots of hydrogen about, e.g. water.

👍 Good source of power.

👎 Takes energy to produce.

👎 Four times as expensive as power from non-renewable sources.

Problem: Solution to global warming

Solution: Technology and 'geoengineering', e.g. scrubbing technology to take CO_2 out of the atmosphere, mirrors in space to reflect solar energy from Earth and reduce the heat.

👎 Very expensive technologies.

👎 Nobody knows what the side effects may be.

Worked example

Explain **one** way in which technology might 'fix' problems of declining resources. **(2 marks)**

Super-efficient cooking stoves have been developed for use in some regions in developing countries. They need less wood to work so help to conserve resources and they produce less CO_2 compared to the normal method of cooking on an open fire.

EXAM ALERT!

This is an excellent answer because one way is correctly identified and then the student goes on to briefly explain why it helps to 'fix' the problem. The second part of the question is the crucial part and many students fail to answer it correctly.

Students have struggled with exam questions similar to this – **be prepared!** ResultsPlus

Now try this

D–C

1 Explain why renewable energy is an important way to resolve resource shortages. **(2 marks)**

2 Outline the difficulties of getting people to:
   (a) reduce their consumption of energy and
   (b) switch to more renewable sources. **(4 marks)**

B–A

Changing employment patterns

The Clark Fisher model shows how employment patterns change as a country develops.

The Clark Fisher model of employment change

1 **Pre-industrial stage**

Most people employed in primary industries (working with natural resources such as farming, fishing and mining).

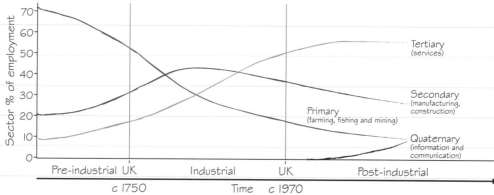

2 **Industrial stage**

- New factories and industries develop providing many jobs, e.g. textiles, steel and engineering goods.
- Chemical and vehicle industries also develop.
- Secondary industries (manufacturing, construction) dominate the economy and employment.
- Tertiary sector (services such as electricity and water) also begins to grow.

3 **Post-industrial stage**

- Tertiary sector provides services to the increasing population who live in towns and cities, e.g. transport, education and health.
- Tertiary sector employment replaces secondary industries in importance.

After the post-industrial stage:
- Employment in the **quaternary** sector begins to grow in importance.
- Quaternary sector is based on research and development and information technology, discovering new products and services.

Worked example
HIGHER B–A

Explain why **stage 3** of the Clark Fisher model of employment change is called the post-industrial stage. **(4 marks)**

When economies have passed through the pre-industrial and industrial stages, they often enter the post-industrial stage. At this point, the tertiary sector, providing services such as transport, education and health, becomes more important than the secondary or manufacturing sector, such as steel, textiles, engineering and chemicals. This is because more and more people are living in towns and are demanding a wide range of services. This pattern was typical of Britain in the 1950s.

Now try this
FOUND G–E

1 Which of the following is the best description of the Clark Fisher model? It shows:

☐ **A** how the employment structure of a country changes as it develops.

☐ **B** the employment structure of a country.

☐ **C** how the employment sectors of a country change.

☐ **D** how tertiary employment increases as secondary and primary decrease. **(1 mark)**

2 Describe what happens in the Clark Fisher model **after** the post-industrial stage. **(3 marks)**

HIGHER B–A

Remember to read the question carefully; it is asking about the period **after** the post-industrial stage.

Employment sectors

You need to know the importance of different employment sectors and working conditions in lower income, middle income and higher income countries.

LICs, MICs and HICs
- LICs: least developed, e.g. Ghana.
- MICs: more developed, where manufacturing industries are developed, e.g. China.
- HICs: higher developed, e.g. USA.

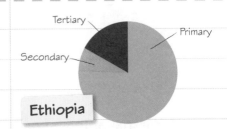

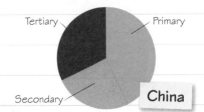

LICs (e.g. Ethiopia)

Primary sector
Dominates! 75% of Ethiopia's population work in agriculture. Most work as subsistence farmers with little commercial agriculture. Long hours, hard physical work.

Secondary sector
Very small! Mainly male employees who work in textile and leather factories.

Tertiary sector
Small! 15% of the population (men and women) work in service industries, including tourism.

Other
Many work in the informal sector – liable to exploitation and abuse.

MICs (e.g. China)

Primary sector
Large! In China, it's the largest sector but is less dominant than in LICs. Includes mining (mostly coal, worked by men), and as farming (often done by women).

Secondary sector
Medium! In China, this sector generates by far the most money. Both sexes work long hours in difficult conditions (often unsafe) but wages are better than in farming.

Tertiary sector
Large! As people earn more money they spend it on services and leisure. Long working hours but good wages and working conditions are better than in factories.

HICs (e.g. UK)

Primary sector
Tiny! Very little fishing or mining. Mechanisation so fewer workers in farming.

Secondary sector
Small! High-tech and highly automated manufacturing remain after relocation of traditional industries.

Tertiary sector
Dominates! Big variety of employment. New ways of working, e.g. working from home, and self-employment are high. A quaternary sector is growing.

Other
Working conditions and pay are good in all sectors.

Worked example

Which of the following is **not** an example of a job in the tertiary sector? **(1 mark)**

☐ A shop assistant
✓ C builder
☐ B doctor
☐ D hairdresser

Make sure you know the different employment sectors.

Now try this

Remember primary industries include mining, farming and fishing.

1 Compare the importance of the primary employment sector to countries at different stages of development. **(4 marks)**

2 Describe working conditions in the secondary employment sector in middle-income countries. **(2 marks)**

Impact of globalisation

You need to know the role of some institutions in globalisation and the impacts of globalisation on different groups of people in the developed and developing worlds.

Institutions

World Trade Organization (WTO), established 1995

Aims to encourage trade between countries and to reduce import duties and other barriers to trade.

International Monetary Fund (IMF), established 1945

Aims to provide the financial stability for trade to flow freely between countries.

> The IMF and WTO have worked together to increase trade and this has speeded up the process of globalisation.

Impact of globalisation

World-wide
- Increase in number of women working (but for less pay than men).
- Improvement in working conditions (i.e. health and safety, working hours, pay).
- Increased skills / training as people move from 'traditional' into 'new' employment areas.
- More goods and services available to everyone.

Developed world
- Wages have improved.
- High prices can be charged for products and services.
- Almost everyone benefits from 'global' goods and services.
- Mostly good working conditions.
- More flexibility and choice in where and when people work.
- Some job losses as companies move to the developing world (e.g. call centres, factories).

Developing world
- Can now sell produce and provide services to a greater number of places.
- Pay high prices for the developed world's services and products.
- Gets lower prices for its products than developed world.
- Wages generally low plus there is continuing exploitation of workers and use of child labour.
- A few who own land / resources have benefited hugely.
- Few people can afford the goods and services a global economy provides.
- Informal sector continues.

Worked example

Describe ways in which men and women benefit from globalisation. **(6 marks)**

Women have received some benefits, for example, more women are now working and therefore getting paid as a result of globalisation. However, women have generally benefited less than men. Women are generally paid less than men and it is mostly men who own and run businesses or land with resources and therefore receive huge amounts of money.

In the developed world, both men and women have benefited from improvements in education and use of the goods and services globalisation provides. However, in the developing world, women are frequently treated as second-class citizens working in poor conditions for little money and receiving little education or training.

> Using words such as 'however' will help you to make comparisons.

Now try this

1 Explain why developing countries get low prices for the products they sell but have to pay high prices for manufactured goods they buy. **(4 marks)**

2 What is the role of the World Trade Organization in globalisation? **(3 marks)**

International trade and capital flows

You need to know the changes in international trade and the flow of capital over the past 50 years.

What has happened?

- International trade has grown hugely (in 2010 it was 48 times larger than it had been in 1970).
- Companies have expanded and invested in countries all over the world (TNCs).
- Banking, insurance and finance companies have also become globalised, offering services all over the world.

See p. 65

For more on this

Foreign direct investment (FDI)

- is the investment which flows from one country to another (often by TNCs)
- may involve buying a business or a factory in the country, or by expanding an existing business in that country
- is done to take advantage of cheaper labour or resources and increase profit.

Some countries offer incentives such as reduced taxes to encourage firms to invest in them.

Reasons why

Transport
Container ships and air transport have made it easier to transport more goods quickly and cheaply.

Communication
IT, e.g. email, text, fax and phone made possible by satellites and undersea fibre optic cables has made communication between countries easier.

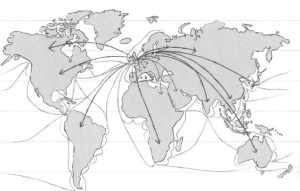

International Monetary Fund
IMF has made it easier for state-led investment in different countries.

Trade agreements
Agreements between countries, e.g. EU, have made trade between countries easier.

TNCs
Growth of TNCs has increased trade between countries.

Worked example

Outline **some** of the main changes in world trade over the last 50 years.   **(4 marks)**

'Outline' means you need to give a few details or write down the most important points.

International trade is now very much bigger than 50 years ago. Transnational corporations (TNCs) have been able to invest more easily in countries all over the world increasing trade between countries. Improved communications have made it easier to conduct business in different countries. The increase in air transport means more goods can be delivered quickly between countries. Larger container ships and supertankers can deliver huge quantities of cargo at one time, cutting costs.

Now try this

1 Describe what is meant by foreign direct investment (FDI).   **(2 marks)**

2 Outline **one** reason for the growth in international trade.   **(2 marks)**

TNCs: secondary sector

You need to know how a TNC in the secondary sector operates in different parts of the world.

What are TNCs?

- Transnational Corporations (TNCs) are large companies which operate in many different countries.
- Over the last 20 years, TNCs have grown in number and importance and cover a wide number of industries.
- Headquarters are usually in a 'global city' in an HIC (e.g. London, New York) with production and selling operations across the world.
- Reasons for going global vary (see spider diagram) but all reasons amount to increasing profits and reducing costs.

to take advantage of incentives   to spread business risk

to be close to markets   **Why TNCs operate globally**   to sell inside trade barriers

to reduce labour costs   to reduce costs of buildings/land

Advantages and disadvantages of TNCs in developing countries

- 👍 Local people are able to earn higher and more regular wages.
- 👍 TNCs bring new skills, e.g. assembly operations and engineering; language acquisition and interpersonal skills.
- 👍 TNCs bring investment, for example in new factories or call centres.
- 👍 TNCs pay taxes which boost the local economy.

- 👎 Pay may be low for workers.
- 👎 Training may only be in low level skills.
- 👎 There may be long shifts.
- 👎 There may be poor working conditions.
- 👎 Some factories may cause air and water pollution.

Worked example

C-B (FOUNDN)

Describe two main advantages for a host developing country of encouraging transnational companies to move production there. Use examples in your answer. **(4 marks)**

The main advantages for a developing country like Malaysia is that local people will be able to earn higher and more regular wages than before. The TNC can bring investment in new facilities, for example, call centres in India. TNCs also pay taxes so this increases the income of the developing country.

EXAM ALERT!

This answer would be improved by adding specific examples of relevant companies. Think about products that you have around the home, do any of these companies operate in different parts of the world?

Students have struggled with exam questions similar to this – **be prepared!** | Results Plus

Now try this

Make sure you read the question carefully. Avoid talking about **advantages** here.

1 State **two disadvantages** for a developing country of encouraging TNCs to move there. **(2 marks)**

E-D (FOUNDN)

2 Using an example you have studied, explain why TNCs in the secondary sector locate some of their operations in developing countries. **(4 marks)**

B (HIGHER)

TNCs: tertiary sector

You need to know how a TNC in the tertiary sector operates in different parts of the world.

How a TNC might operate in the tertiary sector

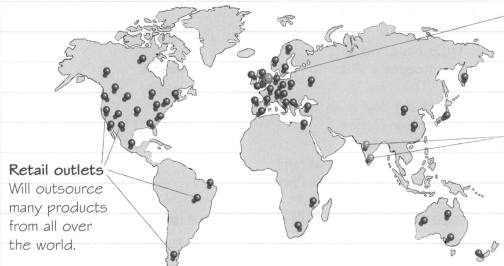

Headquarters in the UK
Employs hundreds of people worldwide.

Customer services
Staff and building costs are very effective.

Retail outlets
Will outsource many products from all over the world.

How tertiary sector TNCs are different to secondary sector TNCs

Tertiary TNCs:

- are often administration companies, especially customer service and call centres, which are relocated to where staff and building costs are cheaper – made possible by modern communications (e.g. internet)

- are often retail outlets (chains) located across the world (secondary sector TNCs have some retail outlets too but are more likely to sell their products to other retailers)

- working conditions are generally better in their overseas offices and shops than in the secondary sector's 'sweatshops'.

Worked example

Explain how TNCs have contributed to the process of globalisation. **(4 marks)**

TNCs have contributed to globalisation in several ways. They are often seen as the 'bridges' that link together the national economies of the world because they operate in different countries. For example, many TNCs, have moved their manufacturing to developing countries where labour and the costs of premises are cheaper but keep some parts of the business in HICs, and some TNCs outsource parts of their business to other companies; both of these increase global trade. Also, many TNCs, such as supermarkets or hypermarkets, have their own retail outlets across the world and / or sell to other outlets, meaning there is a 'globalisation' of products – the same things can be bought everywhere.

> This answer would be improved by the use of relevant examples of TNC companies to support the points made.

Now try this

1 Describe how a TNC you have studied operates around the world. **(4 marks)**

2 Using an example you have studied, explain how a TNC in the tertiary sector operates around the world. **(6 marks)**

What is development?

Development is a term that measures how advanced a country is compared to others. It is about the standard of living in a country – whether people can afford the things they need to survive. However, it's not just about money. Development also includes the quality of life within a country.

Measuring development

The level of development in a country or region can be measured using statistics for **economic indicators** and **social indicators**. Some things such as birth rate are easy to measure but others, such as how safe people feel, are more difficult to quantify but some countries try to do this too. Bhutan measures its Gross National Happiness!

Factors to consider when evaluating development

Economic	Physical wellbeing	Mental wellbeing	Social
• income	• diet	• freedom	• access to education
• type of industries	• access to clean water	• security	• access to health care
• security of jobs	• environment (including climate, hazards, etc.	• happiness	• access to leisure facilities

Economic indicators

- **GDP** – Gross Domestic Product is the total value of goods and services produced by a country in a year. It's often divided by the population of that country to give GDP per capita.

- **PPP** – Purchasing Power Parity adjusts income to take the cost of living in that country into account. For example, $1 can buy a lot more in Sierra Leone than in the USA.

These have limitations because:

- all measures of development show averages only.
- data do not show everything and are not always accurate. For example, GDP doesn't include the cash economy.

Political indicators

Political indicators show what a government is likely to be doing for its country.

- Is it well governed?
- Is there free speech?
- Is there corruption?

Worked example

G-E

Describe **one** example of an economic measure of development. **(2 marks)**

GDP is an economic measure of development. It is the total value of goods and services a country produces in a year.

Now try this

1 Explain some of the problems of **only** using economic measures of development. **(4 marks)**

2 Explain why GDP **per capita** is a better indicator of development than just GDP. **(2 marks)**

The development gap

You need to know some social measures of development and the Human Development Index (HDI). You also need to know the extent of, and changes in, the development gap.

Social indicators

- Birth rate
- Number of people per doctor
- Gender equality
- Life expectancy
- Literacy rate
- Infant mortality

The **Human Development Index** is produced every year by the UN. It's a combined measure of life expectancy, education and GDP per capita which scores each country between 0 and 1:

- 0.8 and over = high development
- 0.5–0.799 = medium development
- under 0.5 = low development.

The development gap

Norway is the most developed country in the world with a score of 0.955.

The standard of living and quality of life in Norway and the DRC are vastly different – the most extreme example of the development gap.

Development is often not continual as many countries regress as well as develop. The 2011 HDI figure for some countries is very similar to what it was in 1980.

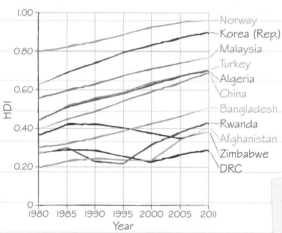

The Democratic Republic of Congo (DRC) and Niger are the least developed countries with a score of 0.304.

The development gap is not really closing between the most and least developed nations.

It's not all bad news as many countries at all stages of development have improved.

Graph of HDI levels for selected countries between 1980–2011.

Worked example

Examine reasons why some countries may stop developing. **(6 marks)**

There may be many reasons why development stops or goes backwards. Natural disasters such as earthquakes, droughts or floods may cause long-term damage to a country. They may affect the infrastructure, the economy and increase disease. Wars can affect all indicators of development as all aspects of life in a country are disrupted. A corrupt government may also hinder development if it stops money and resources going to where they are needed.

Now try this

1 Which of the following **best** describes what the Human Development Index measures? **(1 mark)**

☐ A The number of very rich people.

☐ B People's quality of life.

☐ C The number of hungry people.

☐ D Income variation in a country.

2 Define the term 'development gap'. **(2 marks)**

Development

You need to know a case study of how one country in Sub-Saharan African has developed over time and possible barriers to further progress.

Rwanda

The graph on page 68 shows the changing HDI index of Rwanda since 1980. From this you can tell that development in Rwanda has not been a continuous or smooth process.

1962	Rwanda gained independence from Belgium.
1962–1985	Short outbreaks of ethnic conflict, as well as natural disasters and reliance on coffee as the main crop meant that development until 1985 was slow.
1985–	Development declines as political and ethnic unrest intensifies.
1990	Drought, followed by floods (extending to 2000), wipes out the coffee crop.
1990–	Civil war starts – negatively effects almost all development indicators.
1994	In 4 months, nearly 1 million people (mostly Tutsis) were murdered in genocide. Two million refugees fled the country and nearly 1 million were internally displaced.
1994	A new government is set up and begins to rebuild the country with the help of the UN. Progress is slow as damage is huge and conflict continues in some areas.
2000	A new president is elected. Since then, almost all indicators of development have improved.

Development successes

👍 GDP per capita has grown from $333 to $644 and poverty rates have fallen by 12% between 2006–2011.

👍 Primary school attendance, child mortality and access to clean water have all dramatically improved.

👍 The economy is increasingly divergent and is no longer reliant on coffee (though agriculture is still important).

👍 The government has made development a priority.

Barriers to development

👎 Increasing floods and droughts.

👎 Trade with other countries is difficult because it's a landlocked country.

👎 The possibility of conflict breaking out again is much reduced but still there.

👎 Neighbouring Democratic Republic of Congo is very unstable and there is a risk that conflict may spread and refugees flood into Rwanda.

👎 AIDs and HIV (currently 3% which is low compared to other Sub-Saharan African countries but high by world standards).

Worked example

HIGHER B-A

Using a named example, explain some possible **barriers** to development in a Sub-Saharan African country. **(4 marks)**

An example of a Sub-Saharan country is Rwanda. A possible barrier to continual development is the instability of its neighbour, the Democratic Republic of Congo, which is in the grip of civil war. This may hinder Rwanda's trade with other countries. Also, the conflict may spread across the border which would really set back development. Another barrier is the natural floods and droughts which are increasing.

Now try this

Using a named example, describe the recent **development** of a Sub-Saharan African country. **(4 marks)**

FOUND'N C-B

Try to give examples to support your points.

Theories of development

There are many different theories to explain why societies develop. One of these is Rostow's **modernisation theory** and another is **dependency theory**.

Rostow's modernisation theory

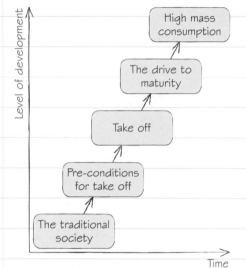

Problems

- It assumes that all countries start at the same level of development.
- It doesn't consider the quality or quantity of a country's resources, population or climate / natural hazards.
- It's out-of-date and based on the 18th- and 19th-century development of European countries.
- It fails to consider that European development came at the expense of other countries (colonisation).

Dependency theory

This is the idea that developing countries can't develop because they are dependent on developed countries. The most developed countries have the economic and political power to exploit less developed countries and impose trade barriers and conditions for loans that hinder development.

Problems

- It was written in the 1950s so is outdated – today, some less developed countries are developing very quickly, e.g. China and India, which may show the dependency theory doesn't work (or only applies to some places).
- It doesn't take account of other factors which may limit development, such as natural disasters, lack of resources, conflict, etc.

Worked example

Explain how Rostow's modernisation theory can help in the understanding of how countries develop. **(4 marks)**

Rostow's theory shows that, over time, countries develop as their incomes rise. It shows that to develop, countries have to meet pre-conditions, such as having educated people to do the work. Once countries have educated people and start saving and investing money, they develop fast. However, this theory assumes development is non-stop so doesn't take account of problems when economies slow down or go backwards.

Make sure you use examples from Rostow's theory to support your points.

Now try this

1 Identify **two** problems with Rostow's modernisation theory. **(2 marks)**

2 Outline why the dependency theory assumes that less developed countries will never develop. **(4 marks)**

Regional disparity

Regions within a country can develop unequally. You need to know the reasons for this and the impacts it can have.

Core and periphery

The **core** is rich and usually urban. This is where big businesses, industries and government have their headquarters. Most people live here and services are good.

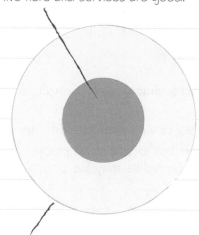

The **periphery** is poor and often rural. It is often where the core gets its raw materials from.

Multiplier effects and downwards spirals

Core regions often have **advantages**, such as:

 fertile soils

🔼 closeness to important markets (trade)

🔼 good communication links

🔼 healthy climate, warm climate

🔼 river / sea ports providing important trade routes.

Periphery regions sometimes have **disadvantages**, such as:

 poor soils

👎 distance from the core and trade routes

👎 difficult communications, especially by road

👎 disease, e.g. malaria

👎 climate hazards, e.g. droughts, floods, etc.

The **multiplier effect** means that core regions get richer and richer as development occurs.

Downward spirals mean that periphery regions become poorer as anyone who can leave, does leave.

Impact of regional disparity

| Lower quality of life in periphery. | → | Conflicts between haves and have-nots. | → | Too many poor people moving to the core. | → | Overcrowding and job scarcity in the core. | → | Slows down development of country. |

Worked example

D-C

Suggest why one region in a country might be richer than another. **(4 marks)**

One region might be a really important port where trade from around the world arrives, creating jobs and bringing in money to the area. The other region might not have any ports or important trade routes. One region might have rich, fertile soils while the other region has poor soils and gets a lot of droughts so it wouldn't be able to grow and sell as much food.

EXAM FOCUS!

In questions like this, remember there are **two** aspects – the poorer region and the richer region. You need to address **both**.

Students have struggled with exam questions similar to this – **be prepared!**

ResultsPlus

Now try this

FOUND'N E-D

1 What is meant by the term 'regional disparity'? **(2 marks)**

HIGHER B

2 Explain **two** problems caused by disparity within a country. **(4 marks)**

Types of development

You need to compare the differences between **top-down** and **bottom-up** development schemes. You also need to know the impacts of a top-down project in a developing country.

Top-down development

National government — External groups (e.g. World bank, TNC's) — Local people

▨ Decision made here
➔ Major influence
➔ Minor influence

- Large-scale projects that usually benefit a country's core area.
- Often very expensive projects and loans often come with conditions attached.
- Projects may not be sustainable and can damage the environment.

Bottom-up development

Outside agencies (e.g. Practical Action, NGOs) — National government — Local communities

▨ Decision made here
➔ Major influence
➔ Minor influence

- Local-scale projects that usually benefit a local / small area.
- Projects cause less environmental damage.
- Usually quite cheap but often local people have to pay for it. Benefits may be short-term.

Madeira River Project – a top-down project

A multinational project in the Amazon area to build four dams to create electricity, a navigation channel and three highways. The area is a peripheral area.

- ✓ 20 000 jobs created.
- ✓ Cheap and affordable electricity to supply energy and increase development.
- ✓ Better communication by roads and river.
- ✓ Expansion of agriculture, e.g. soya bean farming.
- ✓ Flooding minimised by 'run of the river' technology.
- ✓ Two new forest reserves created.

- ✗ 3000 forced to leave their homes.
- ✗ Cost $22 billion.
- ✗ Political problems over flooding of Bolivian territory.
- ✗ Local people didn't want the dams – government forced through plans.
- ✗ More soy agriculture means clearance of rainforest.
- ✗ Disruption of the fishing industry.
- ✗ Environmental Impact Assessment (EIA) for the project was not done properly.

Worked example

HIGHER C–B

Describe what is meant by a 'growth pole'. **(2 marks)**

A growth pole is a centre of development, a cluster of businesses or industries which are growing in a poor region. They are like a mini core and create a periphery within a periphery.

Now try this

HIGHER A

For a named example, explain why a 'top-down' development project has both advantages and disadvantages. **(6 marks)**

Industrial change in the UK

You need to know how the industrial structure of the UK has changed in the past 50 years.

How manufacturing has changed in the UK

1970 — Employment / Contributions to GDP — ☐ Manufacturing ☐ Other
Industries: Iron and steel; Shipbuilding; Textiles

Now — Employment / Contributions to GDP — ☐ Manufacturing ☐ Other
Industries: Electrical; Optical; Motor vehicles

1 Rising wages and rising land prices have made it expensive to produce in the UK and we can't compete with the lower wages and cheaper land from industrial producers in developing countries.

2 There hasn't been enough investment into the industry in order to innovate and develop new high quality products.

3 Automation has meant fewer jobs needed in some industries.

Changes in tertiary and quaternary industry in the UK

There has been a big growth in the importance of tertiary and quaternary industry in the last 50 years.

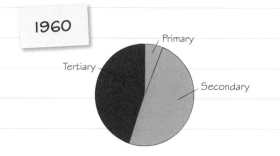

1960 — Primary, Tertiary, Secondary

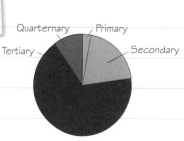

2011 — Quarternary, Primary, Tertiary, Secondary

Tertiary industries (also called service industries), including education, health, retailing, transport and financial services. These have grown with the decline of secondary industries.

Quarternary industries, include high-tech services such as ICT and research. These have grown particularly in the last 10 years because firms are investing more in research departments to develop new products, e.g. mobile phones, computer technologies and robot machinery.

Worked example

FOUND'N E-D

Using an example, explain how government policies have affected **one** industry in the UK.   **(2 marks)**

In 1986, the UK government deregulated financial services. This directly led to the 'Big Bang' – a huge increase in the number of companies that provided financial services such as banks, building societies and insurance companies.

Now try this

FOUND'N D-C

Identify **two** reasons for the rapid recent growth of quaternary industry in the UK.   **(2 marks)**

Make sure you do use a relevant example to help you explain this.

UK employment

You need to know how the UK employment structure has changed over the past 50 years.

Classifying employment

managerial / skilled / semi-skilled / unskilled

male / female

Employment

average wage

full-time / part-time

zero hours contracts

temporary / permanent

Skilled job

Unskilled job

Temporary work
- increase in number
- as a result of the recession, companies reluctant to commit to taking on permanent staff
- contracted staff
- zero hours (an extreme example of temporary work where the worker must be available to work but is not guaranteed hours).

Number of women workers
- varies over time and from place to place
- since 2008, the recession has meant a decline in numbers of women working.

Changes in UK industrial employment

Part-time work
- increase in number
- flexibility for employees
- cheaper for employers.

Average wages
- varies over time and from place to place
- since 2008, the recession has meant only a slow increase in wages.

There has also been an increase in the number of self-employed people, working from home or setting up their own businesses in offices, factories or shops.

Worked example

Explain the possible impacts of changing working practices on employment in the UK.

(8 marks + 3 marks SPaG)

A–A* HIGHER

Three marks are available for SPaG so make sure you leave time to check these and make sure your answer is clear.

In the past few years, one of the most important changes in UK working practices is the rise in flexible working – where people can choose where and when they work. This is possible because of mobile telecommunications and the internet. This had led to more people working from home and a rise in self-employment where people work for themselves. This has several impacts for individuals and businesses. It gives individuals more flexibility which is particularly helpful if they have children or elderly relatives to care for as well as work. For companies, less office space is needed so they may save money by buying smaller premises or won't need to buy bigger offices when they expand. Within offices there is more hot-desking – where people do not have a desk of their own but use any available desk. Also, this should mean a reduction in rush-hour traffic and therefore pollution and CO_2 levels. It will also mean that people do not waste time commuting to and from work – allowing them to work more hours or have more leisure time, as they wish. Finally, it means there are more opportunities for employment in rural areas which should stop people migrating to cities.

Now try this

Identify **one** advantage for staff and **one** for employers of part-time work.   **(2 marks)**

UK regions and employment

You need to investigate the differences in industrial structure and workforce between two contrasting regions of the UK.

North East England versus South East England

North East England

- Industry once dominated by coal mining, iron and steel production, shipbuilding and chemicals but declined rapidly in 20th and 21st centuries due to foreign competition and high land and labour costs.
- The chemicals industry is still important but employs fewer people due to automation and improved technology. It is a centre for biofuel research.
- The Nissan car factory in Sunderland is an important part of the recovery of the area. Other newer industries include the manufacture of North Sea oil and gas platforms.
- Some government departments were relocated to the area.
- Sunderland is becoming a centre for quaternary industry, science and high technology.
- Unemployment is fairly high (10.3% in 2013).

North East

South East

South East England

- Centre for service industries, e.g. health, education and transport.
- Important oil refineries at Southampton.
- New, light industries in the M4 corridor, e.g. electronics and light-engineering.
- Car production, e.g. at Oxford.
- Many financial and business service industries.
- Unemployment is low (6.0% in 2013).

Reasons for the differences
The South East:

- has good communication links to Europe and rest of UK
- has a large pool of skilled and educated people – people migrate to the area from other parts of the UK / world as it provides better job opportunities
- is less affected by decline in industrialisation because there were fewer heavy industries.

Worked example

D-C

Summarise the main changes in employment in one UK region since 1980. **(3 marks)**

There has been a major decline of traditional industries in North East England such as coal mining, steel making and shipbuilding since 1980. But, there is still an important chemicals industry making biofuels, and the growth of car production at Sunderland and new industries such as stem cell research have helped reduce unemployment.

Now try this

Make sure you clearly refer to a specific region.

1 Explain the main differences in terms of employment between **two** contrasting UK regions.
(8 marks + 3 marks SPaG)

2 Outline **two** reasons why industries have chosen to locate in a named region of the UK.
(4 marks)

Environmental impact of changing employment

You need to know the environmental impacts of de-industrialisation and economic diversification in a UK urban area.

Sandwell, West Midlands

In the 1990s, Sandwell experienced industrial decline as many of its manufacturing industries closed. This led to environmental problems, deprivation and poor quality of life.

Problems

By the 1990s

👎 large areas of ground were poisoned by mercury and cadmium

👎 the air was badly polluted

👎 there was very little green space

👎 over 23% of council housing was unfit for habitation

👎 In 1997, Sandwell was the seventh most deprived area in the UK.

Improvement

By 2008

👍 the polluted land had been cleaned up

👍 creation of urban reserves, e.g. RSPB Sandwell

👍 some reclaimed land used for new industries, such as automotive parts

👍 8500 new jobs; 45 km of new roads; 300 new industrial units

👍 new schools had been built or refurbished

👍 the new Midland Metro Tramway increases access to Birmingham and Wolverhampton.

Who helped improve Sandwell?

The Black Country Development Corporation and Tipton Challenge, (paid for by local and central government) 21 Urban Regeneration Companies reclaimed the land and the New Deal for Communities programme helped improve housing and facilities. Sandwell Council is also reducing emissions by 27% and by 2018 aims to reduce them by 45%.

Worked example

HIGHER A–A*

With reference to a named example, explain the environmental impacts associated with deindustrialisation.   **(8 marks + 3 marks SPaG)**

Sandwell in the West Midlands had numerous factories and manufacturing industries but by the 1990s industrial decline had left large areas of land poisoned by mercury and cadmium – a big problem for people's health and the environment. There were large areas of derelict land where industrial buildings and workers' housing had been demolished. Of the remaining housing, over 23% of council houses were classed as unfit for habitation. There were few green spaces. The roads were old and narrow causing traffic jams which added to air pollution. Sandwell became the seventh most deprived area of England.

Now try this

FOUND'N C

Explain how environmental problems caused by deindustrialisation have been resolved in an area you have studied.
          (6 marks + 3 marks SPaG)

Make sure your answer is clear and well-organised and use examples from a specific urban area.

Greenfield and brownfield development

Development can occur on **greenfield** and **brownfield** sites. You need to use examples to compare the costs and benefits of each type of economic development.

Brownfield regeneration

Longbridge, Birmingham

Costs

house prices rising because of demand for the new houses – may mean local people can't afford to live there

neighbouring shops in Northfield losing business

Bourneville College **relocated** into new site costing £66 million

2000 new homes on 468 acre site

Benefits

40 apartments beside park

new hotel

10 000 new jobs

three new green parks created

eases pressure on nearby greenbelt

new shopping centre including a large Sainsbury's and community facilities

In 2011, 98% of house building in Birmingham was on brownfield sites.

Greenfield development

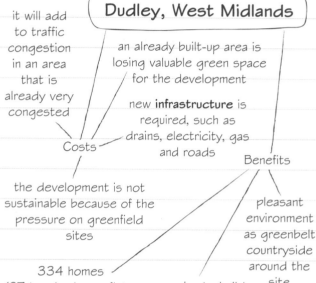

Dudley, West Midlands

it will add to traffic congestion in an area that is already very congested

an already built-up area is losing valuable green space for the development

new **infrastructure** is required, such as drains, electricity, gas and roads

Costs

the development is not sustainable because of the pressure on greenfield sites

334 homes (27 two bedroom flats, 126 three bedroom, 128 four bedroom, 8 five-bedroomed houses) will be built

Benefits

pleasant environment as greenbelt countryside around the site

easier to build on because there are no old buildings to demolish and no pollution to clean up

Worked example

Read the question carefully. Here you are asked about **brownfield** sites only.

Using a named example(s), explain the main **benefits** of developing **brownfield** sites. **(6 marks + 3 marks SPaG)**

At Longbridge in Birmingham, 2000 new homes are to be built, helping to meet local demand for new homes. Bourneville College has relocated there, to a new £66 million facility, and new green parks are being created to bring open green space to a congested area. Most importantly, 10 000 new jobs will eventually be created as a result of the redevelopment. There will be a new local centre including a large Sainsbury's supermarket and community facilities. There will be a new hotel and 40 apartments overlooking the park. Another positive impact of the development is that it eases pressure on the nearby greenbelt.

Now try this

1 Which is the best definition of what is meant by a 'greenfield site'? **(1 mark)**

☐ **A** Land in the countryside.

☐ **B** Land that has been developed before.

☐ **C** Land close to developed sites.

☐ **D** Land that has not been developed before.

2 Using named examples, compare the **advantages** and **disadvantages** of developing brownfield sites. **(8 marks + 3 marks SPaG)**

New employment areas

You need to know about the increasing contribution in the UK of the digital economy, education and research, the 'green' employment sector and foreign workers.

A greener Britain?

EU has pledged to reduce carbon dioxide emissions by 20% by 2020 and to get 20% of its energy from renewable sources, such as wind or water. EU countries (including the UK) have pledged to reduce the carbon footprint of their economies. This should create new jobs in green industries. But will it?

New 'green' jobs

- Renewable energy: wind turbines, HEP, fitting solar panels, etc.
- Water management: reuse, quality and preservation.
- Waste management: recycling.
- Green transport: designers, engineers.

Foreign workers

Recently there's been a big increase in the number of foreign workers in the UK – many from the EU. They often do jobs that many British workers don't want to do or fill skills shortages in areas such as agriculture, industrial cleaning or processing, medicine and health care, construction and building.

The digital economy is set to continue growing as individuals and companies are increasingly reliant on IT technology which already affects most areas of life. This will include new products being developed and services to go with them.

Government and pharmaceutical industries as well as universities are providing increased funding into research for new medical treatments and drugs. This leads to new products which also contribute to the economy as well as people's health.

Growing quaternary sector

Some sectors of the economy (e.g. leisure and entertainment) have already been transformed by the digital economy and others (e.g. health care and financial services) are likely to be transformed in the future.

The growth of colleges and universities into 'businesses' themselves, which develop new products and services in areas such as biofuels, biotechnology, IT and engineering.

Worked example

HIGHER C-B

Explain how the 'green' employment sector may change in the future.   **(4 marks)**

It is difficult to say how the 'green' employment sector is likely to change. Jobs in renewable energy, water management and waste management should increase as the UK tries to become more environmentally friendly. However, many people do not have the skills needed for these jobs and training is not currently in place. Also, some of the work is likely to be done by machines rather than people so there may be fewer employment opportunities than people think. Also, no one knows how popular things such as environmentally friendly transport will become, so that may limit potential job opportunities.

Now try this

1 Outline **one** reason why the 'green' sector is likely to be an important source of new jobs in the future.   **(2 marks)**

2 Explain why the **digital economy** is increasingly important to the economy of the UK.   **(3 marks)**

Urban change in the UK

You need to know the processes that have caused huge urban changes over the past 50 years and why some areas have experienced economic and population growth and others have declined.

 Economic

- **De-industrialisation** – closure of large manufacturing industries often in city centres, e.g. parts of Liverpool.
- New industries – growth of **tertiary** and **quaternary** industries often in rural-urban fringe, e.g. London.
- Prosperity – more disposable income.
- **Wealth gap** – widened leaving pockets of poverty where housing and services are poor and unemployment is high.

 Political

National government policies:
- 1950s / 60s replacing housing with tower blocks
- 1980s Urban Development Corporations to redevelop some places
- 2000s New Deals for Communities – schemes to improve deprived areas.

Local government makes planning decisions and allocates funding. Also maintains communal areas, e.g. roads, parks, paths, leisure/ recreation facilities (frequently linked to health benefits for young and old).

UK urban change

 Social

- Greater **disposable income** and time – growth of leisure and recreational facilities.
- Higher incomes and better transport – move to build housing, work and leisure facilities on rural-urban fringe.
- **Counter-urbanisation** – people moving to rural areas.

 Demographic

- Population growth has meant more housing, services and businesses are needed.
- **Internal migration** – people moving from places with fewer jobs e.g. remote highland areas, to where there are more job opportunities, e.g. London.

Worked example

Try to use an example to highlight your point.

Describe **one** reason why some urban areas have experienced great economic growth over the last 50 years whilst others have declined. **(2 marks)**

Deindustrialisation meant that manufacturing has declined over the last 50 years and tertiary and quaternary industries have grown hugely. Some areas, such as London, have attracted more of this new industry and have grown more than other urban areas, such as Liverpool.

B

Now try this

1 What is meant by the term 'deindustrialisation'? **(2 marks)** F-E

2 Outline **one demographic** process which has caused urban change in the UK. **(2 marks)** B

Had a look ☐   Nearly there ☐   Nailed it! ☐

Changes in urban areas

The processes that have transformed urban areas over the past 50 years have led to variations in the quality of residential areas. You need to be able to examine how these variations have happened and how they have led to some areas of multiple deprivation.

CBD: most expensive land dominated by businesses and services with little housing.

Suburbs: semi-detached and detached housing with more open space and more services, e.g. large supermarkets. Most people living in these areas commute to work.

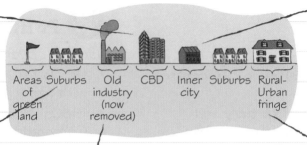

Areas of green land | Suburbs | Old industry (now removed) | CBD | Inner city | Suburbs | Rural-Urban fringe

19th century factories often with terraced housing surrounding the factory for employees. Now either destroyed or regenerated.

Inner cities: former industrial areas that tend to have the cheapest housing with small shops, some services and little open space. Some inner city areas have been developed and contain new housing, services and businesses.

Rural-urban fringe: large, expensive housing, retail parks, business parks and industrial estates and leisure facilities including golf courses, large cinemas, etc.

Causes of change
The different areas of a city / town are caused by economic, social, political and demographic processes. For example, the rural-urban fringe has come about because land is cheaper than in the CBD and there's more space so it's good for businesses. Improved transport and wealth means people can live here because they can travel to work, etc.

Worked example

Explain how some inner cities have become areas of **multiple deprivation**.
(6 marks + 3 marks SPaG)

Most of the UK's deprived areas are in inner cities. These are areas of former industry where factories previously employed the people who lived there. Today, the factories have closed and they have not been replaced by other, low-skilled job opportunities for the people of the area. Unemployment is therefore high which means many people live on very low incomes.

Housing is mostly the old industrial terraces which were poorly built and have a lack of amenities. Some have been replaced with tower blocks where the amenities are generally better but these have led to social problems such as crime and isolation. There is a lack of services in these deprived areas because businesses such as shops and leisure centres don't want to locate to places where they are not likely to make much money. Some areas attract high numbers of immigrants...

EXAM ALERT!

Remember that no urban area is exactly the same as another so be careful not to say **all** inner city areas are deprived or **all** housing in the rural-urban fringe is expensive.

Students have struggled with this topic in recent exams – **be prepared!**   ResultsPlus

Now try this

1   What is meant by the term 'deprivation'?
(2 marks)

2   Give **one** reason why the most expensive housing in urban areas is often located in the rural-urban fringe.   **(2 marks)**

Rural settlements

Rural settlements in the UK have seen great changes over the past 50 years. You need to be able to identify different types of rural settlement and explain how they have changed.

Remote upland communities

Where: e.g. Snowdonia, Scottish Highlands.

Main employment: farming, mining (primary sector).

Population: decline because of loss of primary industries and **pull factor** of urban areas.

Spiral of decline in rural areas

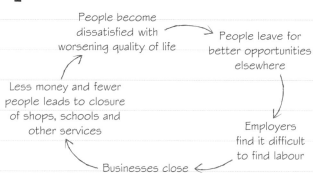

People become dissatisfied with worsening quality of life → People leave for better opportunities elsewhere → Employers find it difficult to find labour → Businesses close → Less money and fewer people leads to closure of shops, schools and other services

Commuter villages

Where: outside the urban fringe but close to towns and cities, e.g. Whittlesford, Cambridgeshire.

Population: increased because people have moved from urban areas and from more remote areas.

Benefits: improved transport links make it easier to travel to jobs in city / town, housing is cheaper and more spacious, safer than cities / towns, access to countryside for leisure.

Disadvantages: decline in services because people use services near to work.

Retirement communities

Where: mainly coastal towns.

Population: large percentage of older people due to older people migrating in and younger people leaving.

Why: people living longer and enjoying good health and want to move away from places of work to more attractive, quieter places with better weather.

Benefits: cheaper housing, specialised services as towns have adapted to ageing population.

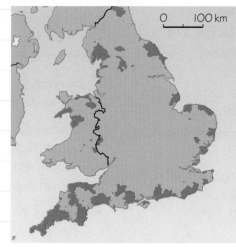

Retirement areas (in orange) are those with a significantly higher than average proportion of people of retirement age and which are experiencing a growth in the proportion of elderly people.

Worked example

Describe **one** characteristic of retirement communities. **(2 marks)**

They are usually towns in rural areas near the coast where winters are mild.

Now try this

1 Which **one** of the following types of settlement has become **smaller** over the past 50 years? **(1 mark)**
☐ A Commuter villages.
☐ B Settlements in the rural-urban fringe.
☐ C Remote upland villages.
☐ D Retirement communities.

2 Outline **one** reason why commuter villages have expanded over the past 50 years. **(2 marks)**

Contrasting rural areas

Just like urban areas, rural regions of the UK can be very different in terms of **quality of life** and **deprivation**. You need to know examples of two contrasting rural regions in the UK.

North Wiltshire

81% rural but six towns contain around 60% of the population – steady population increase and economic growth.

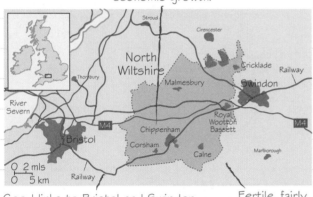

Good links to Bristol and Swindon and 75 minutes to London.

Fertile, fairly flat land with mild climate.

Scottish Highlands

Only Inverness has a population of over 10 000 people. Generally, the lowest population density in the UK (less than 0.1 per person per hectare). Except for Inverness, there is a declining population.

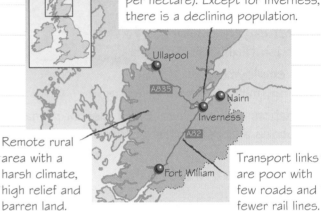

Remote rural area with a harsh climate, high relief and barren land.

Transport links are poor with few roads and fewer rail lines.

Quality of life

- Unemployment is low and is spread across a range of industries.
- High proportion of public sector and low wage jobs.
- Good accessibility allows people to commute for work if need be.
- Access to medical, educational and retail services is good – though car dependant.
- Loss of services in smaller settlements but services are good in larger ones.
- Growing population is putting a strain on some services.
- Affordable housing shortage for people who work and live in the area because of commuters and second home ownership.

Quality of life

- Unemployment is low but available jobs are few and mainly in the primary sector.
- The remoteness and relief of the area means that there are very few industries and businesses.
- The economy is almost totally dependant on agriculture and tourism and therefore vulnerable.
- Service provision is poor and totally car dependant.
- There is a declining and ageing population with many young people leaving for where there are greater opportunities.
- Access to beautiful countryside for leisure and recreation.

Worked example

Define 'quality of life'?
(2 marks)   **HIGHER C**

Quality of life is a measure of happiness. It is usually made up of things such as job security, living conditions, health and so on.

Make sure you know the key geographical terms.

Now try this

1 Outline **one** reason why many remote areas of the UK have **declining** populations.
(2 marks)   **FOUNDN E–D**

2 Using named examples, examine the differences in quality of life in **two** contrasting rural areas of the UK.   (8 marks + 3 marks SPaG)   **HIGHER A–A***

Impact of housing demand

You need to know the rising demand for housing in one urban area. You also need to know how some of these demands are being met through **urban regeneration** projects.

Impacts of rising demand

By 2020 around 3 million more homes will be needed in the UK due to growth in population, more households (more living alone) and increased wealth. This housing demand will have several economic, environmental and social impacts.

Improving urban areas

Renewal strategies
- **Regeneration** means 'growth'. Urban regeneration projects try to improve the economy, housing and services of an area.
- **Rebranding** an area means giving it a new image so that it will attract businesses and development.

Impacts of increased housing

Environmental	Social	Economic
• More waste, emissions, traffic and pollution during building and when lived in. • Building on greenfield sites inevitable.	• Strain on existing services, e.g. schools, hospitals and leisure facilities • Existing home owners may resent new residents.	• Expensive and it can take time for investors to get a return on their money. • The real need is for low-cost housing but this isn't very profitable.

Worked example

HIGHER A-A*

Using named examples, examine the **impacts** of rising demand for housing in an urban area of the UK.
(8 marks + 3 marks SPaG)

London is an example of an urban area in the UK which is experiencing a big housing shortage. Lack of housing means that house prices and rents are very high, which affects less well-off people the most. It also means that some housing areas are very overcrowded so they are not very nice places to live. This can be bad for the environment because of the pollution and waste produced. Overcrowding also puts pressure on public utilities such as water and sewage as well as on services such as medical and leisure facilities. A social...

To do well you would need to explain further impacts in detail. Think about the social, economic and environmental impacts.

London Docklands regeneration project

👍 24 046 new houses (including low-cost) and old housing improved.

👍 2700 businesses including Canary Wharf providing over 85 000 jobs.

👍 New health, education and leisure facilities and shopping centres.

👍 Improved transport links, e.g. Docklands Light Railway, link to MI, City airport.

👎 Some don't like the changes because of a loss of a close-knit community and lack of jobs for the unskilled.

Now try this

1 What is meant by the term 'urban regeneration'?
(2 marks)

FOUNDN D-C

2 Outline **one** way regeneration projects can help improve urban areas.   **(2 marks)**

HIGHER C-B

Making rural areas sustainable

You need to know examples of strategies to improve rural areas and evaluate their success.

Rural development schemes

1 The England Rural Development Programme (2007–13) invests money in non-farming activities.

3 The expansion of **broadband** internet to remote areas increases business opportunities although needs further development.

Helping rural businesses and stopping the migration to cities

2 Regional Development Agencies give grants to enterprises and support development.

4 EU's **Convergence Objective** invests in rural businesses such as the Eden Project which now provides 400 jobs and attracts over a million visitors every year, boosting the local economy.

Rural planning policies

Conserving the countryside

- **Green belts:** have strict building controls and stop urban sprawl around cities and towns. They cover 13% of England.

- **National Parks:** are managed by the National Park Authority (NPA) which restricts development in Parks. It also manages footpaths and visitor centres and aims to limit environmental impact.

Effects

Green belts and National Parks have both positive and negative effects on the economic development of rural areas.

👍 Green belts have slowed down urban sprawl and restricted development.
👍 National Parks have preserved beautiful landscapes.
👍 NPA policies have encouraged tourism and leisure bringing economic development.
👍 Green belts and National Parks are enjoyed by locals and tourists.

👎 Some areas of green belt have been developed in spite of planning rules.
👎 Visitors to National Parks and green belts can damage the environments.
👎 There's a lack of affordable rural homes, which cannot be built in National Parks or on most green belt land.
👎 It is often difficult to build house extensions or set up a business.

Explain how successful National Parks are in managing the environment and economic needs of developing rural areas.

(6 marks + 3 marks SPaG)

 Three marks are available for SPaG so make sure these are really good, that your answer is well-organised and aim to use geographical terms.

National Parks have been very successful in helping the environment by preventing building developments within the Parks. However, this has led to housing shortages. It is also difficult to set up new businesses, which can affect the economic development of the area. The NPA successfully encourage visitors by providing facilities such as visitors centres. The centres are successful in contributing to the local economic development. However, the number of visitors can damage the landscape – eroding footpaths and leaving litter. This is a big problem in very popular National Parks such as the Peak District which is close to cities like Sheffield and Manchester.

 C-B

Outline **one** way that rural development schemes can benefit rural areas.   **(2 marks)**

Global trends in urbanisation

The world's population is becoming increasingly **urbanised** and cities in developing countries are growing at a particularly fast rate.

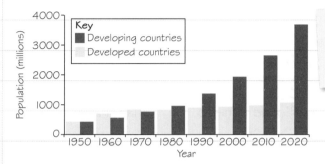

The growth of urban population in developed and developing countries.

Urbanisation in the UK, a developed country

1750
Impact of industrial and agricultural revolutions – people moved to the cities to find work in the new factories as less labour was needed in the countryside. Towns grew at a rate of 10% per year.

1900
Towns and cities continued to grow as a result of **rural depopulation**.

2012
80% of population live in towns/cities.

Due to some movement back to the countryside for a better quality of life, some towns and cities are shrinking slightly. However, some places such as Birmingham continue to grow as younger people want to live in the centre (**re-urbanisation**).

Urbanisation in developing countries

This urban growth has similarities and differences to the developed world.

By 2010, there were 23 **megacities** (urban areas with over 10 million inhabitants). Over half were in developing countries.

Similarities
- Movement of people to the cities because fewer jobs in the countryside due to mechanisation (**push factor**).
- More jobs available in cities and towns and better facilities, e.g. electricity, piped water and health care (**pull factors**).

Differences
- Speed of urbanisation much faster.
- High fertility rates in city populations (families have many children) has been a major factor in increase of population.
- Better conditions has meant the birth rate is higher than the death rate.

Worked example

Explain why most of the future growth of cities is likely to be in the developing world. **(4 marks)**

Cities in developing countries are growing much faster than cities in developed countries where few urban areas are experiencing any increase in population. In developing countries, the urban population is growing because of natural increase – the birth rate is higher than the death rate. There is also migration from rural areas to urban areas (urbanisation). Many people are moving to the cities because agricultural practices are becoming more mechanised and there are fewer jobs, so people move to cities for work. Drought or other natural disasters may also force a move. Generally, urban areas provide people with better living conditions, such as piped water, electricity and health care, and higher wages.

Now try this

Compare the growth of cities in developing countries with that of cities in developed countries. **(8 marks + 3 marks SPaG)**

Megacities

You need to know the differences in megacities in the developed and developing world.

Megacities – world cities with populations over 10 million

Examples of megacities:

Developed world	Developing world		
Paris	Sao Paulo	Karachi	Lagos
New York	Cairo	Mexico City	Mumbai
Istanbul	Dhaka	Delhi	Shenzhen
Moscow	Beijing	Rio de Janeiro	Shanghai
Los Angeles			

Differences

Megacities in developed world
- May have government buildings.
- Headquarters (HQ) of TNCs, stock exchanges.
- Financial firms and other service industries dominate.
- Cultural institutions, e.g. opera and ballet.
- Large tourist industry.
- Efficient transport systems, e.g. metro.
- Less heavy industry and manufacturing.

Megacities in developing world
- Dominated by manufacturing industries.
- Some service industries.
- Fewer TNC headquarters.
- Fewer cultural institutions.
- Very little tourism.
- Cover vast area.
- Informal housing.
- Poor transport systems.

Spatial growth of cities

Developed world

Central Business District (CBD) – shops, offices, government buildings at centre

Suburbs – residential (houses), supermarkets, retail parks

Inner city – mixture of old decaying housing and factories and brand new developments

Key
- CBD
- Inner city
- Suburbs

Developing world

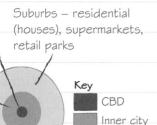

Key
- CBD
- Expensive housing
- Cheap and medium-price old housing
- Modern factories
- Squatter settlements

High-quality commercial spine develops

Differences
- No defined land use areas. Fast growth and weak planning controls lead to irregular layout.
- People set up homes on any patch of land they can find because there is such a shortage of houses. These become spontaneous or squatter settlements, with mostly slum housing which quickly grows into shanty towns.
- Richer homes built along main roads.

Worked example FOUNDN D-C

State **one** difference in the economic activities in megacities in the developed and developing worlds. **(2 marks)**

Megacities in the developing world have a large informal sector (unrecognised employment) where people work for themselves on the streets selling things or providing services such as shoe cleaning. This is far rarer in developed world megacities.

You need to be specific about the difference – give an example.

Now try this

Describe the differences in the spatial growth of megacities in the developed and developing world. **(4 marks)**

Urban challenges: developed world

You need to know about the challenges facing towns and cities in the developed world.

Cities in developed countries

Works out how much pollution is generated by burning coal, oil and gas

Works out how much land is needed to provide a city with all its energy, water, food and waste disposal

Measures the impact of cities on the environment

Eco-footprints

Calculated by scientists

Explained in terms of how much land per person is needed to support the city. In the UK, the average figure is 5.3 hectares of land per person

Works out how much land is needed to absorb the pollution and waste created by the city

A busy street in York

York's eco-footprint – the challenges

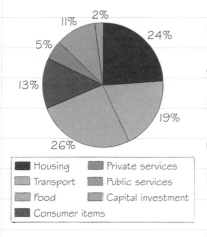

2%
11%
24%
5%
13%
19%
26%

- ■ Housing
- ■ Transport
- ■ Food
- ■ Consumer items
- ■ Private services
- ■ Public services
- ■ Capital investment

1 Food – most is imported from abroad or brought from other parts of UK which uses a lot of energy in transport and packaging.

Challenge – to import less food.

2 Energy – for heating, cooking, washing, etc., the demand for energy rises as more people live in the city.

Challenge – to waste less energy.

3 Transport – car ownership is more popular than public transport.

Challenge – to cut down on pollution and congestion.

4 Waste – expensive and difficult to dispose of.

Challenge – to cut down on waste.

Worked example

Describe **one** challenge facing cities in the developed world. **(2 marks)**

Demand for water in many cities in the developed world is far greater than supply. This is because of a high level of usage – people living by themselves and using appliances which consume large amounts of water (e.g. dishwashers). Places where water is stored is usually far away from these cities.

Aim to use words such as 'because' to help you fully describe your point.

Now try this

1 Explain why large cities in the developed world have a large eco-footprint. **(4 marks)**

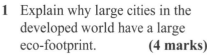

2 Explain the challenges facing cities in the developed world. **(6 marks + 3 marks SPaG)**

Urban challenges: developing world

The three main challenges for cities in the developing world are: informal housing (slums), pollution and lack of jobs. All these lead to a low quality of life for those living in the cities.

Slums and shanty towns (squatter settlements)

Homes built from scrap materials on any spare land because there is no other housing available

Dangers from fire, flooding and landslide

There is no clean water, electricity, rubbish collection or organised sewage disposal

Life in the shanty towns is very stressful

Slums and shanty towns

Crime rates are high

Litter and sewage creates a breeding ground for disease

People are malnourished because there is a lack of money and food

Pollution

Traffic congestion and poorly maintained cars generate serious air pollution, creating health problems. A dense smog can cover the whole area of Mexico City

Supplies of underground water beneath some cities is being used up so fast that the land on the surface is sinking. Mexico City has sunk 7 m in the last 100 years

Pollution

Rivers and seas are used as dustbins, destroying wildlife

As the cities spread outwards, wildlife habitats are destroyed as well as agricultural land

Lack of jobs

- Most people work in the informal sector because there aren't enough formal jobs for everyone. People will set up their stall on the street and sell food, fruit and vegetables, cut hair, sell water, carry luggage, take photographs, etc.
- Only a few people have jobs in the formal sector in factories or offices with regular pay and other benefits.
- The work can be unreliable and badly paid with no benefits or security.

Worked example

Outline **two** reasons why squatter settlements are found in cities in the developing world. **(4 marks)**

The cities are growing so fast that there are too many people for all the proper housing in the city so people just build their own shacks and basic shelters wherever they can. This also happens because of a lack of planning laws. In any case, many people who move to the city cannot afford to pay rent for a proper house so could not move to one even if more houses were available.

Now try this

1 Which of the following is an example of a job in the informal sector of the economy? **(2 marks)**

☐ **A** Selling goods in a shop.

☐ **B** Polishing shoes.

☐ **C** Serving food in a restaurant.

☐ **D** Selling goods found on rubbish tips.

2 Explain **one** cause of pollution in cities in the developing world. **(2 marks)**

Reducing eco-footprints

You need to know how one city in the developed world is reducing its eco-footprint. The city of York has made efforts to reduce its **eco-footprint** in the following ways.

Saving energy

- ✓ Turn down the thermostat.
- ✓ Shower rather than have a bath.
- ✓ Use a washing machine on low-heat cycle.
- ✓ Dry clothes outside rather than using a tumble dryer.
- ✓ Fill kettle only for what you need.
- ✓ Wait for a full load for the washing machine.
- ✓ Turn off lights when they are not needed.
- ✓ Close curtains at dusk to conserve heat.
- ✓ Turn off rather than use stand by.
- ✓ Choose the right size pan for your cooking.

Reducing waste

- ✓ Households, shops and businesses to sort recyclable waste into paper, textiles, plastic, glass and cans.
- ✓ Offices to use less paper and more electronic forms of communication.
- ✓ Over 70% of the methane generated from landfill sites is now recovered and used.
- ✓ People are encouraged to buy fewer pre-packaged goods to reduce the volume of household waste.

Sustainable transport

- ✓ Park and ride scheme.
- ✓ Bicycle lanes.
- ✓ City car club – cars available for hire.
- ✓ Car sharing.
- ✓ Traffic-free pedestrian zone.

Reducing imports of food

- ✓ Monthly farmers' market selling only food produced within a 40 mile radius.
- ✓ Specialist markets: Made in Yorkshire crafts.
- ✓ Edible York is a group with community vegetable plots around the city.

These schemes encourage people to:
- buy local produce
- grow own produce
- buy goods with less packaging.

Worked example

Using a named example, explain ways in which a developed world city can reduce its eco-footprint.
(6 marks + 3 marks SPaG)

You need to know how one city in the developed world in reducing its eco-footprint.

York has managed to reduce its eco-footprint in several ways. The local council advises people on how to reduce their energy use, for example by turning off electrical equipment when it is not being used or turn down the heating. It also advises people on how to reduce their water use, for example by fixing dripping taps or having a shower instead of a bath. It offers a good recycling service for households so less waste is produced. Also, 70% of the methane generated from landfill sites is used to make electricity. York has also introduced many schemes to make transport more sustainable, such as a park and ride scheme and a pedestrian zone, which encourages people to leave their cars out of the city centre and use public transport.

Now try this

Describe the main benefits to **(a)** people and **(b)** the environment of reducing York's energy consumption.
(4 marks)

Strategies in the developing world

There are many ways in which developing world cities are trying to improve the quality of life for people who live there and reduce pollution.

Curitiba, Brazil – a sustainable city

In 2010, the city was awarded the Globe Sustainable City Award which was set up to recognise cities and urban areas which excel in sustainable urban development.

The city has preserved its green spaces, with 28 parks and wooded area. Builders get tax refunds if their projects include green space and new lakes now absorb flood waters which were a problem in the past.

Children can exchange recyclable garbage for school supplies, food and chocolate. So 70% of the city's garbage is recycled.

Bus transport system is used by 85% of the population. The system is fast, cheap and efficient and transports 2.6 million people each day. The buses use alternative fuels such as natural gas which creates less pollution.

People living in low-income areas bring their rubbish to collection centres and swap them for bus tickets and food. This means there is less litter and disease.

Retired buses are used as mobile schools or offices.

NGOs

Non-governmental organisations (NGOs) try to improve the quality of life for people in cities.

- Urban Green Partnership Programme helped to create 300 home gardens in Sri Lanka which helps local people feed themselves as well as adding green spaces to urban areas.
- Centre for Urban and Regional Excellence has provided a simple waste water and sewage plant which means this doesn't pollute drinking water supplies in Kachpura, India.

Worked example

Examine the **advantages** and **disadvantages** of attempts to make a city in the developing world less polluted. **(8 marks + 3 marks SPaG)**

Mexico City is trying several measures to reduce pollution. The government has provided a fund for spare parts to repair and improve buses in the city. The advantages are that this reduces the air pollution produced by buses as well as improving their reliability so more people are likely to use the bus rather than a car. The disadvantage is that the buses are already old so they will wear out soon and the parts are expensive. Another measure to try and reduce car use and therefore air pollution is banning drivers from using their cars one day per week. This has reduced the amount of cars on the road slightly but people get around the system by buying another car.

Mexico City is also trying to reduce water pollution by building more sewage-treatment plants which has reduced pollution but are expensive to build. People also try to store rainfall in tanks so less water has to be pumped from aquifers which is very cheap, however, this water is polluted by animals and insects so does not really solve the problem.

To do well you would need to add one more advantage and one more disadvantage. For example, pumping water from deeper wells.

Now try this

Using example(s), explain how some cities in developing countries have improved the quality of life for the people who live there. **(6 marks + 3 marks SPaG)**

Rural economies

You need to know about the rural economies of both the developed and developing world.

Services
- Shops, pubs, garages
- Schools and doctor's surgeries
- The smaller the population, the fewer the services

Developed rural economy

Employment
- Employment in farming, forestry, mining, fishing and quarrying in decline
- Recreation, tourism and running services provides some jobs
- Increasing number and type of businesses (due to broadband, transport etc).

Agriculture
- Mostly large and commercial farms
- Highly mechanised and intensive
- Small, family farms in decline.

Agriculture
Subsistence farming
- Very small, family run
- Low productivity
- Little mechanisation

Cash crops
- Owned by large companies
- Grown for export e.g. rice, fruit
- Crops grown to be made into other products e.g. biofuels
- Intensive with growing mechanisation

Developing rural economy

Employment
- Vast majority in agriculture where wages are low (or non-existent)
- Recreation and tourism provides some jobs
- Very few employed in services as it's so sparse

Services
- Usually very few services
- Some shops
- Few schools

Farming systems

Arable farms grow crops.

Pastoral farms raise animals for meat, milk or wool.

Mixed farms do both.

What is farmed depends on physical factors (e.g. climate) and human factors (e.g. machinery available).

	Subsistence farms	Commercial farms
Inputs	Low tech / high labour	High tech / low labour
Outputs	Small, family use only	Large, sold for profit

Worked example

B

Suggest **one** advantage and **one** disadvantage of cash crops for rural areas in developing countries. **(4 marks)**

One advantage is that farms growing cash crops in developing countries employ thousands of local people giving them an income. One disadvantage is that many cash crops are only grown for export so local people cannot buy them which can be very unfair when there are food shortages.

Now try this

1 Which of the following is an example of a cash crop?

G-E

☐ A Eggs
☐ B Fish
☐ C Roses
☐ D Milk   **(1 mark)**

2 What is meant by 'commercial farming'?

C-B

(2 marks)

Rural challenges: developed world

In developed countries, rural areas are changing mainly due to urban and **demographic** processes which create many challenges. You need to examine these challenges for a named rural area.

Rural depopulation – better opportunities and services in cities as fewer jobs in farming.

Development – pressure on 'real' countryside from house building.

Tourism pressures – **honeypot** locations swamped by visitors.

Rural challenges

High house prices – caused by second home ownership and commuters make it difficult for local people to buy a home.

Decline in services – less services needed because of depopulation, commuters and second home ownership.

Challenges by rural type

The four types of rural area in the developed world have some different challenges depending on how close to cities they are.

Commuters may use the services in the urban area where they work rather than those near their home. Local services, e.g. shops and bus links, may close or stop but they need to be maintained for the people who don't commute.

Within a daytrip range of a big city, the challenges include: managing tourism and recreation 'honeypots' to benefit as many people people as possible; create jobs and affordable houses for those young people who do stay in the countryside.

Remote countryside
Accessible countryside
Commuter belt
Urban fringe
URBAN AREA

As this area suffers from **rural–urban** migration, the biggest challenge is to reduce this by creating jobs for young people. Other challenges include isolation and managing tourism opportunities to benefit local communities.

Threat from **urban sprawl**. Conflict between preserving countryside and providing new homes and work places.

Worked example

Using a named example, explain some of the **challenges** in rural areas in the **developed** world.   **(6 marks + 3 marks SPaG)**

Snowdonia is an area of remote countryside in Wales which faces many challenges. Firstly, there is increasing rural depopulation as local people are moving away. A major reason for this is lack of jobs in Snowdonia. Many people who live there work in primary industries such as quarrying and farming. Some quarries have shut or reduced their labour force and agriculture is struggling with competition from abroad. There is also a lack of housing which means house prices are high and local people cannot afford to live there. Also, many houses are holiday homes or second homes. As more people move away, local services, such as shops, do not get enough business so have to close.

Check that your spelling, punctuation and grammar are really good and that your answer is clear.

Now try this

1 Using an example, describe what is meant by the term 'honeypot'.   **(2 marks)**

2 Describe how second homes can cause problems for rural areas in the **developed** world.   **(2 marks)**

Rural challenges: developing world

In developing countries, rural areas face many challenges which are often linked to a range of physical and human processes. You need to identify these challenges for a named rural area.

Human hazards, such as HIV/AIDS, malaria, cholera, TB and wars mean less people to work the land.

Rural–urban migration – many people (especially young men) are moving to urban areas attracted by jobs, wages and services.

Land degradation from **desertification** and **deforestation** has led to decline in fertile areas.

Rural challenges

Population growth puts increased pressure on the land leading to land degradation.

Globalisation, e.g. multinational mining companies and commercial farming, often does not benefit local people in rural areas.

Natural hazards, such as floods, droughts and earthquakes, increase the death rate as well as damage the land and crops that grow on it.

Rural Kenya

- 50% of Kenya's population is poor.
- Rural–urban migration means farming workforce mostly old and female.
- Some land is rich, but poor farming techniques, land ownership problems and land degradation mean overall yields are low.
- Commercial farming takes the best land and produces food for export.
- 75% of Kenya's poor are rural
- High rate of HIV / AIDs.
- Few jobs except subsistence farming.

A rural settlement in Kenya

The spiral of decline in rural areas of some developing countries

Food insecurity → Rural–urban migration → Neglect of farming → Less food produced → Food insecurity

Worked example

Explain why people in rural areas of the developing world often want to move to urban areas. **(2 marks)**

People want to move to urban areas for better jobs because in rural areas subsistence agriculture is the main job. Rural jobs do not pay much money, if any, but urban jobs mean that a person can send money home to their family.

Now try this

1 Outline how rural–urban migration can cause problems for rural areas in the **developing** world. **(2 marks)**

2 Using a named example, explain some of the challenges facing rural areas in the **developing** world. **(8 marks + 3 marks SPaG)**

Rural development projects

Different groups try to improve livelihoods and opportunities in rural areas in the developing world. You need to know about the roles of these groups and some initiatives they run.

NGOs – charities which raise money to set up and run development projects.

IGOs – intergovernmental organisations (e.g. the UN) use funds donated by individuals and governments.

Local communities raise money through donations and business partnerships to fund their own small-scale projects.

Who helps?

National governments of the developing countries use tax payers' money to fund projects. These are usually on a large, national level.

Local governments use funds given from national government to fund smaller-scale projects.

Development projects: Ethiopia

Ethiopia

Koraro – cluster of 11 villages helped by the NGO, Millennium Promise. Providing:
- 3 micro dams, 30 safe water points
- resources to improve school classrooms
- bed nets with insecticide coating to help prevent malaria
- training for farmers on ways to plant crops and use fertilisers which has led to better crop yields.

Afar region – a drought-ridden, very poor area where farmers are often helped by the NGO, FARM-Africa. Providing:
- irrigation systems so crops get a reliable water supply
- seeds to grow crops farmers can sell for money
- loans so farmers can invest in new seeds or tools (micro-finance).

Ways to improve the quality of life and economies in rural areas in developing countries

- Better transport – buying and selling produce, assessing services.
- Fresh water and sewage treatment – irrigation for crops and clean water means less disease.
- Electricity – makes life easier and better, providing heat, light and power.
- Education – schools, teachers and resources for children and adults (adults given training in agricultural techniques and health care, etc.).

- Improved communications – use of mobile phones to better connect rural areas to urban areas.
- Improve access to health care – mobile health services travelling to remote areas.
- Micro-finance – loans and other finance given to small rural businesses (that don't have access to banking services) so they can improve and expand.

Worked example

C-B

What does the term 'NGO' mean?
(2 marks)

NGOs are non-governmental organisations. These are charities or other organisations which are independent from any government and are funded by donations.

Make sure you know your geographical terminology.

Now try this

1. Outline **one** way in which the quality of life in rural areas in developing countries could be improved. **(2 marks)**

2. Describe **one** benefit of improving access to education in rural areas in developing countries. **(2 marks)**

Developed world: farming

The farming economy in the developed world needs to adapt so that it can become more sustainable. You need to know examples of how this can be done.

Making farming economically sustainable

1 What farmers can produce
- 'New' animals, e.g. alpaca, ostriches, deer, bees.
- Own products, e.g. make cheese, yogurt, honey, bottled water.
- 'New' crops, e.g. organic, biofuels, herbs.

2 Where farmers can sell
- Farmers' markets.
- Farm shops.
- Pick your own.
- Specialist food retailers.

3 How farmers can diversify
- Holiday accommodation.
- Leisure activities, e.g. fishing, clay pigeon shooting.
- Converting buildings to cafes, restaurants, offices.
- Leasing land, e.g. wind turbines.

Making farming environmentally sustainable

Method	Why's it more sustainable?
Arable rotation	Instead of growing grain every year (which takes a lot of nutrients out of the soil), grow legumes like peas or beans occasionally as this returns nitrogen to the soil.
Organic farming	Instead of chemical fertilisers, pesticides, genetically modified crops, weedkiller and animal feed which contains antibiotics and growth hormones. Organic farming uses crop rotation, green manure, compost and biological pest control.
Drip irrigation	Instead of spraying water onto crops, this uses computers to control flows of water through pipes to water plants directly to their roots which saves a lot of water.
Hedgerows	In the 1960s and 1970s hedgerows were grubbed up to make huge fields that big machines could farm efficiently. But the fields were not sheltered and lost lots of topsoil to wind and water erosion. Hedgerows provide shelter, keep livestock where you want them and are home to many animals, insects and birds.

Worked example

FOUNDN D-C

Outline **one** way that farming in the developed world could be made more environmentally sustainable. **(2 marks)**

One thing that makes farming unsustainable is exhausting the land by growing only one type of crop on it year after year. Mixing bean rotations into the farming system every few years returns nitrogen to the soil.

Now try this

HIGHER A-A*

Examine how farms in the **developed world** could become more economically and environmentally sustainable.
(8 marks + 3 marks SPaG)

Developing world: farming

You need to know examples of how intermediate (also called appropriate) technology and fair-trade schemes can help make farming in the developing world more sustainable.

Examples of intermediate technology

Improving water supplies for irrigation	Improving soil quality and reducing erosion
Digging boreholes to access water deep underground.	Planting trees to conserve moisture and reduce soil erosion.
Recycling sewage water in shallow lagoons.	Recycling solid human waste for fertiliser.
Building small dams on rivers.	Contour ploughing and / or building low walls to reduce soil movement.
Conserving rainwater in barrels or trapping it behind stones and trees.	Turning slopes into terraces to reduce soil erosion and increase land that can be used.

Intermediate technology

> Equipment is accessible for local people because it isn't expensive to buy or maintain and it doesn't require much training to use.

↓

> Improves water supplies and reduces soil erosion improves soil quality/ thereby increases yields.

↓

> Makes farming **economically sustainable** and protects environment so makes farming **environmentally sustainable** too.

Fair trade

- Producers are paid an agreed minimum price plus a premium to be invested in local community projects.
- Working conditions are checked.
- Gives farm owners / workers and local communities more money to help increase economic sustainability.
- Monitoring makes sure fair trade is environmentally sustainable too.

2% Farm workers in producing country

33% Wholesale and retail

10% Farmer's profit, fertiliser and transport costs

20% Ripening, importer's costs and advertising

35% Storage and shipping costs

> Who gets the money spent on non-fair trade bananas?

Worked example

FOUND^N D-C

Explain how farming in developing countries can be made more sustainable. **(6 marks + 3 marks SPaG)**

One way to make farming in developing countries more sustainable is by using intermediate technology to increase yields so farmers make more money. This means using equipment that is cheap to buy and look after and local people can use easily. An example is digging boreholes so farmers can access water that is deep underground for irrigating crops. Another example is...

Now try this

HIGHER C-B

Describe how fair trade benefits farmers in the developing world. **(4 marks)**

To do well you would need to extend this answer with more examples of how farming could be made sustainable.

Unit 3

Unit 3 is about making careful and well thought-out **decisions** based on evidence.

Pulling it all together

This is a synoptic unit. This means it **links** and interrelates topics from across Units 1 and 2.

You need to make sure that you have a very thorough understanding of the **core topics** in Unit 1 (Physical) and Unit 2 (Human) and the links between them.

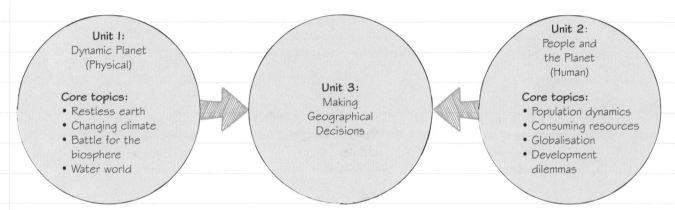

You will use the skills and knowledge you have developed and draw all this together to **analyse** a geographical problem. You will then consider, select and justify possible **solutions**.

Before you begin

You will be given a source booklet which contains maps, diagrams and written resources. You will need to use the information in the source booklet and **your own knowledge** to answer the questions in the exam.

Spend around 20 minutes reading, analysing and making sense of the sources in the resource booklet **before** you start to answer the questions.

The exam

Your Unit 3 exam will last 1 hour and 30 minutes and is worth a total of 53 marks. You will need to answer **all** the questions.

The final question will ask you to make a decision based on the sources and your own knowledge. There will also be 3 marks available for **spelling**, **punctuation** and **grammar** so make sure that you check these, that your answer is well-organised and that you use geographical terminology correctly.

Introduction

In your Unit 3 exam, you need to make **decisions** based on evidence about topics that affect our planet.

Key ideas

Your Unit 3 paper will be on **one** topic. The topic will cover one or more of these key ideas:

Physical processes and environmental changes increasingly put people at risk

Investigating organisations' attitudes towards the concept of sustainability

Achieving sustainable development requires funding, management and leadership

Key ideas

Balancing the needs of economic development and conservation is a difficult challenge

Defining sustainable development and evaluating styles of development to assess whether they are sustainable

Demand for resources is rising globally but resource supply is often finite which may lead to conflict

Oil supplies in the USA

On the next 11 pages, you will be able to revise the skills needed to tackle your Unit 3 exam.

In the exam, you may have more sources and more questions than here.

The context for this section of the revision guide is: **'The future oil supplies of the USA'**.

Now try this

Look over the core topics you covered in Units 1 and 2.
Make short notes on:
(a) developments linked to oil
(b) wilderness areas
(c) environmental protection
(d) energy demands of the developed world.

Remember, you need to use your own knowledge from Unit 1 (Physical) and Unit 2 (Human) as well as the sources in your Unit 3 exam.

Looking at sources

The five Ws

Use the 5 Ws to help you analyse sources.

1 **What** is it? What is it about? What does it show?

2 **Why** was it taken / written / produced?

3 **Who** is it giving information about? Who are the people in it?

4 **Where** was it taken / written / produced?

5 **When** was it taken / written / produced? (How long ago, what time of day, etc.)?

Top tips

When reading a source, always:

- read captions carefully
- **underline** key words
- identify **links** with Units I and 2
- make short notes on any **trends** in graphs or **features** in photographs
- note any **differences** or **conflicts**.

Have a look at this source to see the 5 Ws in action.

What? A newspaper report about the building of a controversial pipeline.

Why? Because Daryl Hannah is a film star and was arrested whilst protesting about an environmental issue.

Where? In Texas, in the USA.

Daryl Hannah arrested in Texas protesting pipeline

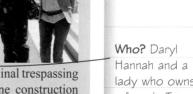

Film star Daryl Hannah was arrested Thursday afternoon for protesting at the construction of a major oil pipeline in Texas. The Keystone XL pipeline is designed to bring crude oil from Canada to Texas' Gulf Coast. Hannah and 78-year-old Texas landowner Eleanor Fairchild were arrested for criminal trespassing after they were accused of standing in front of pipeline construction equipment on Fairchild's farm in Winnsboro, Texas. Ms Hannah said, "I was peacefully protesting the advances of Trans Canada on Eleanor Fairchild's land. They insist on bullying her and taking away her land." She is concerned that the pipeline may break and damage important natural environments such as the Ogallala Aquifer, which supplies water to many US farms. Trans Canada responded by saying that their pipeline will be the safest in North America. They believe the pipeline will have various benefits, including boosting the economy.
(October 2012).

Who? Daryl Hannah and a lady who owns a farm in Texas.

When? In 2012, when the construction of the pipeline was underway.

Worked example

Explain the two main reasons why Daryl Hannah was protesting in Texas. **(4 marks)**

Daryl Hannah was protesting about the building of a pipeline to carry oil from Canada to the USA. She is worried that the pipeline might break and so pollute the water in the Ogallala Aquifer. This water is used by farmers in the USA so this would be a disaster. Secondly, she was protesting because the landowner in Texas, Eleanor Fairchild, does not want the pipeline to cross her land but the government has forced her to sell the land.

Now try this

Which of the following is Daryl Hannah suggesting? **(2 marks)**

☐ **A** That the pipeline should go ahead.

☐ **B** That the government should force Eleanor Fairchild to sell her land.

☐ **C** That the pipeline might pollute the water supply.

☐ **D** That the pipeline should be moved to another location.

Section 1: Oil supplies in the USA

Your source booklet will always start by giving the background to the problem. Have a look at the sources below, then look at the worked example on the next page.

Background to the problem

How should the USA develop its future oil supplies?

- Some people think that the US should aim to produce more of its own oil supplies.
- Others believe that the US should reduce its reliance on oil and use more renewable energy.
- Still others believe that the US should look to secure future oil supplies from friendly nations nearby.

The government of the United States must make a decision about the future.

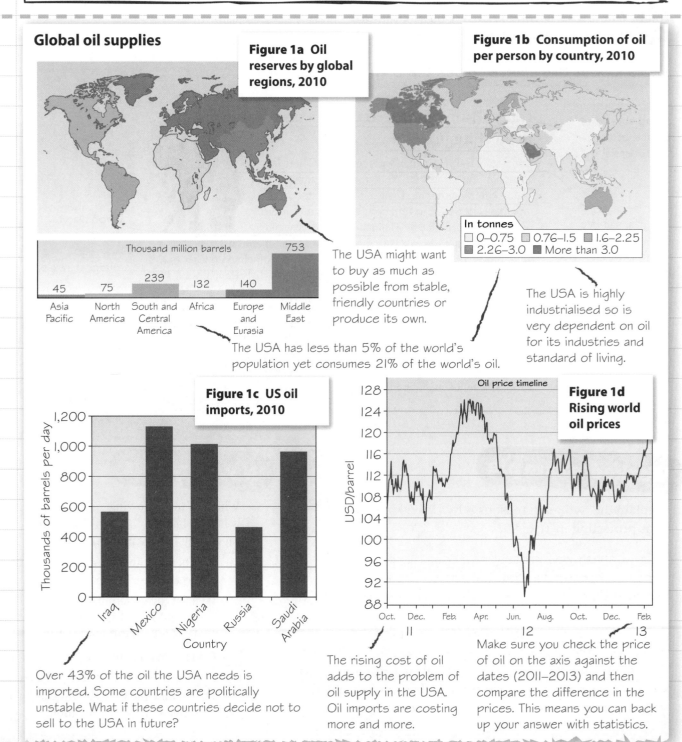

Global oil supplies

Figure 1a Oil reserves by global regions, 2010

Thousand million barrels

Asia Pacific	North America	South and Central America	Africa	Europe and Eurasia	Middle East
45	75	239	132	140	753

Figure 1b Consumption of oil per person by country, 2010

In tonnes
- ☐ 0–0.75
- ☐ 0.76–1.5
- ☐ 1.6–2.25
- ☐ 2.26–3.0
- ☐ More than 3.0

The USA might want to buy as much as possible from stable, friendly countries or produce its own.

The USA has less than 5% of the world's population yet consumes 21% of the world's oil.

The USA is highly industrialised so is very dependent on oil for its industries and standard of living.

Figure 1c US oil imports, 2010

Thousands of barrels per day

Country: Iraq, Mexico, Nigeria, Russia, Saudi Arabia

Figure 1d Rising world oil prices

Oil price timeline

USD/barrel

Oct. Dec. Feb. Apr. Jun. Aug. Oct. Dec. Feb.
11   12   13

Over 43% of the oil the USA needs is imported. Some countries are politically unstable. What if these countries decide not to sell to the USA in future?

The rising cost of oil adds to the problem of oil supply in the USA. Oil imports are costing more and more.

Make sure you check the price of oil on the axis against the dates (2011–2013) and then compare the difference in the prices. This means you can back up your answer with statistics.

Section 1: Oil supplies in the USA

Figure 1e Three views on America's future oil supplies

Martha Brook, US House of Representatives: 'Doing nothing is not an option. We must increase the supply of oil to the USA. Renewables will not be able to produce enough energy to meet the demand.'

Lester McDonnell, Chief Executive Canco Oil (Canadian oil): 'We have large oil reserves in Alberta, Canada. We can get to export our oil to the USA, which gives them regular, safe supplies from a friendly country.'

Jody Kahn, Campaign Manager for Environment USA: 'Natural wilderness areas which are important and we must protect them, not pollute them. The wildlife in these areas is of world importance. We should rely on renewable energy not on drilling for oil.'

Worked example

1 (a) Study Figure 1c. Which countries provide most of the oil imported into the USA? **(1 mark)**

Mexico and Saudi Arabia.

First, look for the country from which the USA imported the most oil. Write it in your answer then cross it off the source. Then look for the next country, and so on.

(b) Outline why these are the most important suppliers of oil to the USA. **(4 marks)**

Use the data on page 99 and find evidence about the need to import oil from countries that are close and friendly. This is a good chance to use synoptic and reference skills.

The USA wants to import as much oil as possible from countries that are close to its borders. This is because oil can be difficult and expensive to transport so it is cheaper to import oil from countries near to the USA, and Mexico and Canada both share a border with the USA. The second reason why these three countries supply most of the USA's imported oil is that they are friendly to the USA and are not likely to cut off oil supplies. This is also true of Saudi Arabia, which is a friendly nation in the Middle East and a supporter of the USA.

2 Describe the increases in the world oil price since 2011? **(2 marks)**

The world price of oil has increased from about $106 a barrel in October 2011 to over $119 a barrel in February 2013, so it has increased by over $13 per barrel. It was even more costly in March–April 2011 before the start of the Euro crisis.

Now try this

Study the opinions of the three people in Figure 1e. Outline why oil supply is a challenge for the United States. **(3 marks)**

101

Section 2: Developing new oil resources 1

Drilling for oil may be a possible solution for the USA. One area where this might be possible is the Western Arctic Reserve (WAR) of Alaska. It is important to consider the economic and environmental costs and benefits of oil development in wilderness areas.

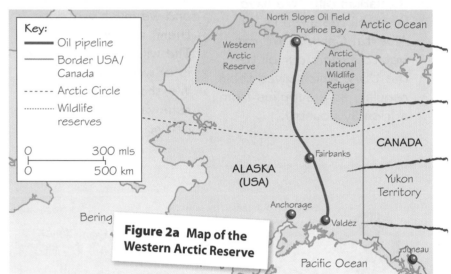

Figure 2a Map of the Western Arctic Reserve

Key:
— Oil pipeline
— Border USA/ Canada
- - - - Arctic Circle
.... Wildlife reserves

0   300 mls
0   500 km

North Slope Oil Field
Prudhoe Bay
Arctic Ocean
Western Arctic Reserve
Arctic National Wildlife Refuge
CANADA
Fairbanks
ALASKA (USA)
Yukon Territory
Anchorage
Valdez
Bering
Juneau
Pacific Ocean

The North Slope Oil Field and a pipeline carrying oil to the ice-free port of Valdez are already in place, so these will not need to be built.

The pipeline runs beside two wildlife reserves.

The technology for drilling in these extremely cold environments already exists so the companies have expertise in minimising oil pollution from drilling and pipelines.

There is already a route for tankers to take the oil from Valdez to the rest of the USA.

Figure 2b Key facts about the Western Arctic Reserve (WAR)

- In 1923, the US government designated the WAR an area of strategic oil and gas reserves which the nation could use in the future, for example in a time of emergency.
- The area consists of two ecological regions. **The Arctic coast** to the north consists of pristine wetlands, coastal lagoons and grass meadows. It is home to 25% of the world's Pacific Black Brant Goose population. It is a summer habitat for millions of migrating birds, together with moose, caribou, wolves and polar bears. **The Brooks Range** of mountains has the highest numbers of peregrine falcons, gyrfalcons and rough legged hawks in the world. It has the largest herd of caribou (430 000) in Alaska.
- There is little environmental protection in WAR, only a few 'special areas'.
- The cost of drilling for oil in the WAR are high (in the region of $33 billion).
- 40 000 tonnes of oil waste come from each rig. Oil drilling in the WAR could amount to 50 000 tonnes of extra nitrogen dioxide.

Think about the human issues involved, for example, the WAR was set up as an area for use in times of national emergency. If this is now developed, the USA will have lost this safety net for any future times of trouble. Are there other things that can be done to meet the country's oil needs without developing the WAR?

Figure 2c The Brooks Range of mountains, Alaska

Think about what you've learned about global warming. Nitrogen dioxide is an important greenhouse gas

Section 2: Developing new oil resources 1

Worked example

1 Identify **three** pieces of evidence from Figures 2a and 2b which show that the WAR is an important area for biodiversity.   **(3 marks)**

The northern part of the WAR is the Arctic coast. This is a region of wetlands, coastal lagoons and grass meadows. In contrast, the second region is mountainous. The northern region provides habitat for 25% of the world's Pacific Black Brant Goose population whilst the Brooks Range is home to moose, caribou and polar bears. The northern region is a summer habitat for millions of migrating birds whilst the Brooks Range has the largest herd of caribou (430 000) in Alaska.

Keep answers as accurate as possible and include examples and specifics facts. Use your own words rather than using a chunk of text from the resource.

Worked example

2 Outline **two** possible threats to the environment of drilling for oil in the WAR.   **(4 marks)**

One important threat to the environment is the destruction of wildlife habitat by drilling for oil in the WAR. The variety of wildlife, such as gyrfalcons, found in the two ecological regions are of world importance and damage to the habitat of these creatures could be a serious blow to their survival.

A second threat is the increase in global warming that would result from drilling for oil in the WAR. Anything that adds to global warming would be an important threat to the world environment.

Remember, you need to summarise and synthesise (pull together) the information from different sources.

Worked example

3 Study Figure 2c then answer the questions.

(a) Explain why drilling for oil or building pipelines across this area might be difficult and expensive.   **(4 marks)**

This is an area of steep slopes, high mountains and few roads, so it would be difficult to get drilling equipment into the area. It would also be difficult and expensive to try to build a pipeline because they would have to drill through the mountains and find ways to support it across the deep valleys.

(b) Suggest why building pipelines or drilling for oil on the lowland area might also be a problem.

The lowland areas might also be a problem because in spring, when the snow melts, the areas might flood roads, the pipeline and drilling rigs.

Now try this

Examine the main advantages of drilling for oil in WAR.   **(4 marks)**

Make sure you refer to the photographs and map as well as the text.

Section 3: Developing new oil resources 2

The USA could acquire oil resources by building a pipeline from areas in North America, such as the tar sands of Alberta, Canada. Think about the balance between the costs and benefits.

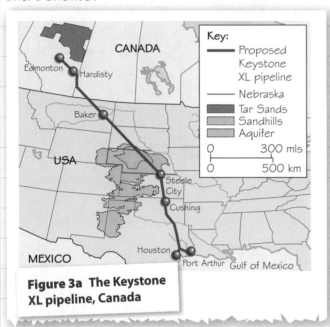

Figure 3a The Keystone XL pipeline, Canada

Key:
— Proposed Keystone XL pipeline
— Nebraska
▨ Tar Sands
▨ Sandhills
▨ Aquifer

0 ——— 300 mls
0 ——— 500 km

CANADA
Edmonton
Hardisty
Baker
USA
Steele City
Cushing
MEXICO
Houston
Port Arthur Gulf of Mexico

Figure 3b Key facts about the US Keystone XL pipeline

- A pipeline could run from the tar sands to the oil refineries on the US Gulf Coast.
- It would cross the Ogallala Aquifer and Nebraska Sandhills (one of the largest sand dune formations in the world).
- Up to 100 000 people would be employed building and operating the pipeline.
- It would provide 5% of US oil needs and save 9% of US imports.
- US states along the route would receive extra tax revenues.
- The cost of building the pipeline would be around $7 billion.
- An estimated 180 billion barrels of bitumen may lie in the tar sands.

| 1. Extracting tar sands by open cast mining is easy because the layers are close to the surface.

Overlying peat bog and forest must be cleared. | → | 2. Large volumes of water are needed, so water diverted from local rivers. | → | 3. Crusher chews up oil sands into smaller pieces. | → | 4. Tar sands mixed with heated water. Heating uses large volumes of natural gas. Burning the gas adds to global warming by creating a lot of carbon dioxide (possibly 12-17% more than conventional oil production). |

7. Polluted water pumped into open-air ponds. Some polluted water can leach back into the water table. ← 5. Tar (bitumen) separates from sand and water.

6. Bitumen refined to produce oil.

This will have a negative environmental affect. Peat bog can't be renewed easily. Habitats would be destroyed.

Waste water may pollute local rivers, which supply drinking water.

Figure 3c Tar sand extraction diagram

Extracting the oil uses a lot of water and natural gas, so will be expensive. Also contributes to greenhouse gas emissions.

Figure 3d The Ogallala Aquifer

These valuable water supplies could be affected by possible oil spills. What would the human, environmental and economic costs be?

- The Ogallala Aquifer sits underneath eight US states and provides water for 2 million people.
- Over 27% of all US irrigated land depends on it.
- It supports some of the most productive farmland in the USA.
- There is not enough rainfall in the area to support large-scale commercial agriculture.

Section 3: Developing new oil resources 2

Worked example

C

1. Outline **three benefits** of developing the US Keystone XL pipeline.   **(6 marks)**

The main benefits of developing the US Keystone XL pipeline are the increase in employment of up to 100000 people, who would be engaged in building and operating the pipeline. In addition, US states along the route would get extra tax revenues. However, more importantly this solution would provide 5% of US oil needs and save 9% of US imports, and so reduce dependence on imported oil. It would also mean that the USA would not need to drill for oil in the WAR.

Look at the key facts about the pipeline on page 104 and the map of the pipeline. Think about possible social and economic benefits and also think about what you have learned in Units 1 and 2.

Worked example

A

2. Examine the main environmental **costs** of developing the US XL Keystone pipeline.   **(8 marks)**

The environmental costs would include damage to the Sandhills of Nebraska, an area of 50000 sq km of wetland and home to 314 species of vertebrates including mule deer, red fox and coyotes. There may also be pollution of the Ogallala Aquifer. This is one of the world's largest aquifers, covering 450000 sq km, and over 27% of all US irrigated land depends on it. This is an extremely productive farmland area. If the water supply were polluted, the effects would be disastrous as there is no alternative source of water. Crops and animals would die and food would have to be imported from other countries. There could also be environmental damage in the tar sands area of Alberta (Canada). Extracting the oil is difficult and expensive because it needs large volumes of water and natural gas. Mining here may destroy the forest and peat bog, which currently cover the area. These are sensitive environments prone to damage from pollution. Burning the natural gas to extract the oil would add to greenhouse gases by creating a lot of carbon dioxide.

In an 8-mark question like this, you would need to bring in some of your knowledge from Units 1 and 2 as well as using source evidence. Think about extreme climates and pollution, as well as global warming and its effects.

Pollution of the Athabasca River and the water it supplies to surrounding areas could also be mentioned.

The question refers to the environmental costs so try to focus only on this.

Now try this

Describe some of the ways farmers could adapt to the shortage of water in the Ogallala Aquifer.
     (4 marks)

Section 4: Renewable energy

This section looks at some of the costs and benefits of renewable energy for the USA.

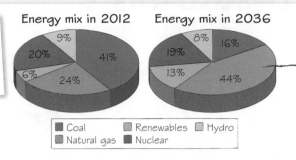

Figure 4a How the USA intends to develop its energy provision by 2036

Energy mix in 2012   Energy mix in 2036

This is a good opportunity to think about what you may have learned in Units 1 and 2 about sources of energy. What are renewable resources? What are recyclable resources?

Legend: ■ Coal   ■ Natural gas   ■ Renewables   ■ Nuclear   ■ Hydro

---

Lee Black, Chair US nuclear forum: 'Solar power relies on sunshine, just as wind power relies on the wind blowing. So, there are times when these simply will not produce enough energy to meet the rising demand in the US. Renewables have had lots of investment but have only produced a small amount of expensive extra power. So in the short term, we still need oil, gas and nuclear power.'

Erin Riley, spokesperson for US renewable energy: 'Renewable energy does not pollute the atmosphere and that is very important. In future, we may not need as much oil as now because the US is working hard to help firms and people to reduce the amount of oil and energy they use by funding and promoting projects such as longer-lasting light bulbs and better insulation of homes.'

Figure 4b Two views on renewable energy

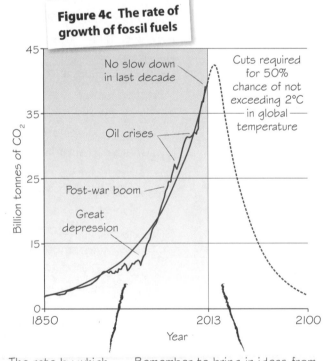

Figure 4c The rate of growth of fossil fuels

No slow down in last decade

Cuts required for 50% chance of not exceeding 2°C in global temperature

Oil crises

Post-war boom

Great depression

Billion tonnes of CO$_2$

1850   2013   2100

Year

The rate by which use would have to drop in order to meet fossil fuel reduction targets.

Remember to bring in ideas from Units 1 and 2. For example, the USA didn't sign the Kyoto Agreement so the country is not strongly committed to reducing the use of fossil fuels.

… BP has abandoned some initiatives in renewable and low-carbon energy, withdrawing from the solar industry and dropping its investment in the development of carbon capture and storage technology. Bob Dudley, BP's chief executive, said last month that the company had 'thrown in the towel on solar' after trying to make money at it for 35 years.

Figure 4d Adapted from *Financial Times*, April 3rd, 2013

Major oil companies are moving away from renewable energies such as solar power because they do not see that they have a big future in the USA, and they are not profitable.

Section 4: Renewable energy

Worked example

FOUND'N D

1 Study Figure 4a then answer the questions.
  (a) By how much are renewables planned to increase by 2036?
  7%
  (b) By how much is the use of coal planned to change by 2036? **(3 marks)**
  Reduce by 25%

> Look at the general trend shown in graphs, as well as the percentages.

Worked example

HIGHER C-B

2 Explain what the terms **renewable** and **non-renewable** mean in relation to resources. **(3 marks)**

Renewable resources include solar, wind and water power, which renew themselves indefinitely and give continuous supplies. Non-renewable resources include coal, oil and natural gas as well as minerals such as copper and iron. They cannot be remade because it would take millions of years for them to reform. There is a fixed amount of non-renewable resources and they are gradually being used up.

> This is a good chance to refer back to what you learned in the core topics, for example Topic 2 on Consuming resources. Make sure you are clear on the key terms, such as renewable resources etc.

Worked example

HIGHER B

3 Study Figures 1b and 1c on page 100. Describe the pattern of oil reserves in relation to oil consumption. **(5 marks)**

The Middle East has the largest oil reserves and also one of the highest consumptions of oil. North America has one of the highest consumptions of oil but small reserves. Africa and South / Central America have low consumption of oil but higher reserves (particularly South / Central America). Asia Pacific has low consumption of oil (apart from Australia) and small reserves. Europe, including Russia, has high consumption of oil and quite large reserves (mostly in Russia).

> Look closely at world maps (like the ones on page 100) as they will give a lot of data which you should use.

Worked example

4 (a) Outline **two** advantages of the USA relying on renewable energy in the future. **(4 marks)**

  (b) Outline **two** disadvantages of the USA relying on renewable energy in the future. **(4 marks)**

(a) There will be less pollution of the environment and global warming will slow down because there will be less carbon dioxide in the air.

(b) Some developments such as solar power and wind power depend on the elements and there are many places in the country which do not have enough sunshine or wind to make these forms of energy a replacement for oil, especially when the demand for oil is rising. In addition, these developments are expensive to put into practice.

Now try this

Study Figure 4d. Suggest **one** reason why oil companies are moving out of solar energy.

(2 marks)

Options

The final section of your exam paper will present a number of options. You need to make a decision and choose **one** of the options for which you need to argue a case.

Option 1: Drill for oil in the WAR

It would be possible to drill for oil in the Arctic coastal area of Alaska, in the area called the Western Arctic Reserve (WAR).

Things to think about:
- there is already an oil field in the North Slope development, so the technology for drilling in a hostile environment already exists
- there is an existing Trans-Alaska Pipeline, built in the 1970s to carry oil across Alaska to the port of Valdez, so any new oil could use this
- the USA would be less reliant on imported oil
- there is a route for oil tankers to take oil from Valdez to the rest of the USA in place already
- the oil companies have learned a lot about minimising pollution from oil drilling and oil pipelines
- there could be environmental damage as a result.

Option 2: Build the US Keystone XL pipeline

The USA could bring oil from the tar sands of Alberta, Canada, via a new pipeline to the USA.

Things to think about:
- there are very big reserves of the tar sands in Alberta, Canada
- this would provide 5% of US oil needs and save 9% of US oil imports
- it would create jobs
- those US states along the route of the pipeline would each get extra tax revenues from the new pipeline
- the US would be getting oil from a friendly neighbour rather than a potentially hostile nation
- there could be environmental damage as a result.

Option 3: Develop more renewable sources of energy

The USA is working to develop even more renewable sources of energy such as solar, wind, geothermal and wave power so may not need as much oil in the future.

Things to think about:
- the US would save a considerable amount of money by not drilling for oil in the Arctic and by not building the pipeline (over $40 billion)
- there would be less environmental damage in the USA and Canada
- the US is working hard to help firms and people to reduce the amount of oil and energy that they use by promoting and funding projects such as long-lasting light bulbs and better insulation of homes
- the demand for oil continues to rise in the USA and the cost of oil also continues to rise
- it is questionable whether renewables will be able to meet the future demand for energy
- the attitude of oil companies to investment in renewable energy.

Options

Worked example

HIGHER A–A*

Study the three options for the USA

1 Select **one** option you think would be best for the environment and for the United States. Justify your choice.
 • Use information from Units 1, 2 and 3 to support your answer.
(12 marks + 3 marks SPaG)

I think the pipeline would be the best option. This is because a lot of people would get jobs and US states along the route would get more tax. It would also save the USA having to import so much oil.

I don't think that the environmental costs are a big problem. The Ogallala Aquifer does not appear to be a very important area for wildlife. The amount of carbon dioxide created might add to global warming but so far the changes to climate have been small.

The drilling for oil in the WAR is not a good option because the roads and drilling pads would pollute the wilderness environment...

Try to be specific and say how many jobs or how much oil.

*Here links could be made to previous knowledge. For example, how oil leaks from the pipeline could be prevented (by better monitoring sensors). Try to link to Unit 1 and global warming and make sure your statements can be supported with **evidence**.*

Make sure you discuss the advantages and disadvantages of your chosen option to help explain why you think this is the best option.

Remember that 3 marks are available for SPaG, so make sure that your spelling, punctuation and grammar are really good and concentrate on spelling key words correctly.

Try to give specific examples to support your points. For example, the impact on caribou could be mentioned.

Worked example

FOUNDN C

2 Select **one** option you think would be best for the people and the environment of the USA. **Choose from options 1 and 2**.

Explain the advantages and disadvantages of this option for the USA and its people.
 • Use information from the resource booklet and your knowledge from Units 1 and 2 to support your answer.
(9 marks + 3 marks SPaG)

I think the USA should drill in the Western Arctic Reserve (WAR). The main advantage would be that the USA would have the oil it needs to support its industries and to power its transport systems. It would also reduce dependence on imported oil (43% of its needs) from countries which may become unfriendly. This will mean the USA is more secure.

The disadvantages are the dangers to wildlife, but I think these are often exaggerated and the companies could try to avoid damage to ecosystems ...

Make sure you explain the advantages and disadvantages of your chosen option.

It is good to give statistics of imports. Try to also mention recent rising costs of oil from Figure 1d. Support your argument with examples, such as evidence from the sources of how much oil could be produced and how much imports could be reduced.

The section on potential environmental damage would need more detail and examples of the potential risks. Detail of which ecosystems and which wildlife and how they would be affected would be useful. Remember to use your knowledge from Units 1 and 2 as well.

There are 9 marks available for this answer (plus 3 marks for SPaG), so make sure that you take time to answer the question fully.

Now try this

Select **one** of the partial student answers above and in the light of the comments, write an improved version to score full marks.

Think about using a clear structure for your answer. Link your points and explain each one carefully. Use examples and your own knowledge to help present your argument.

Answers

UNIT 1: DYNAMIC PLANET

Restless earth

1. Moving tectonic plates
1 Crust, mantle and core.
2 Deep cracks open in the crust and magma rises to the surface to form a ridge.

2. Plate boundaries, volcanoes and earthquakes
1 Four from: at destructive plate margins, two plates collide; where an oceanic plate meets a continental plate; the denser oceanic plate sinks beneath the continental plate – the subduction zone; the edge of the continental plate buckles, causing fold mountains to form; earthquakes occur due to the friction between the two plates; melting of the crust creates molten magma which rises to the surface forming volcanoes.
2 Three from: between the top of the Pacific Plate and the North American Plate; between the Nazca Plate and the South American Plate; between the African Plate and the Eurasion Plate; between the Pacific Plate and the Indo-Australian Plate; between the Philippines Plate and the Eurasian Plate.

3. Volcanic and earthquake hazards
1 The amount of damage and devastation from a volcanic eruption varies with:
  - the type of volcano – shield volcanoes are likely to be less explosive but lava flows a long way, causing damage to buildings and farmland in its path; composite volcanoes are violently explosive – lava will not flow so far, but the eruption will also contain gases and ash which may cover a wide area and cause damage to farmland and buildings, poisonous gases for animals and humans, etc.
  - location of volcano – if closer to urban areas likely to cause more damage than those in remote areas
  - how vulnerable the place is – more developed countries are better protected and have better warning systems, etc., than less developed countries.
2 High-speed 'avalanche' / flow of a mix of ash, gases and rock which erupts from a composite volcano.

4. Managing earthquake and volcanic hazards
1 Any two from: animals and birds may move away from the area; gas emissions which can be measured show an increase; there is a rise in the temperature of the soil; the sides of a volcano may swell; there my be a lot of small earthquakes; water supplies in the area may be cut off and the water may contain more minerals.
2 Any three from: volunteers enlisted to help with all the injured people and to clear away the debris; storage or plans to access clean water to prevent the spread of disease; access to additional food supplies because often shops, towns, roads and farms have been damaged; ways to communicate by radio because phones will often not work; medical help to care for the injured people; a plan to evacuate the area if needed.

5. The Haiti earthquake
1 Any suitable case study could be used. For Haiti, any two from: about 310 000 deaths; huge number of injured and dead trapped under rubble; power lines down; communications not working; roads blocked by rubble or destroyed; nearly 300 000 buildings destroyed (or had to be demolished).
2 Any two suitable case studies could be used but ideally should be one from a developing and one from a developed country. For Kashmir in 2005 and Loma Prieta in 1989:
  - people died and were injured in both earthquakes but far fewer in Loma Prieta (63 dead, 3757 injured) than in Kashmir (75 000 dead, 75 000 injured)
  - buildings were damaged in both and people were made homeless but again this was far worse in Kashmir because of the poor-quality housing – 2.8 million made homeless in Kashmir compared to 12 000 in California

  - transport networks, for example roads, were damaged in both
  - cost of damage in Loma Prieta exceeded that in Kashmir by a lot because of the more expensive infrastructure and buildings that had been damaged – $440 million in Kashmir compared with $10 billion in Loma Prieta
  - additional hazard in Loma Prieta as clay soil liquefied causing gas mains to burst and fires.

6. Volcanic eruptions
1 Any two from: be ready to move out at short notice; practice evacuating the area; watch the volcano for signs of smoke and lava; be aware of any earthquakes occurring locally.
2 Use a suitable case study and provide specific details (facts and figures). Any two from: deaths of people/animals; destruction of property due to lava or ash; destruction of farmland due to lava, ash or poisonous gas; evacuation of people; disruption to transport routes – roads / rail / rivers could be covered in lava or ash; flooding caused by blocking rivers / lakes; fires caused by poisonous gas.

Changing climate

7. Past climate change
1 One from: changes in the Earth's orbit; changes in the Sun's output; volcanic activity; changes in ocean currents; large asteroid collisions.
2 A period of thousands of years when it is colder than usual so there is more ice coverage.

8. The impact of climate change
1 Megafauna evolved to live in cold conditions – when temperatures rose they couldn't adapt to warmer conditions and became extinct.
2 Two from: ice core records; fossil record; pollen record; tree ring data; coral reef samples; coastline changes; glaciation record on the landscape, etc.

9. Present and future climate change
1 Steel production.
2 Any two from: carbon dioxide, methane and nitrous oxide.

10. Climate change challenges
1 You need to include at least three of the following with two in detail: average temperature likely to increase due to rise in global temperatures; amount of rainfall likely to change and be less predictable – shift in the North Atlantic Drift and more cyclonic, stormy weather due to change in air masses from the north; winters may become colder due to more Arctic air masses; change in timing and length of the seasons, etc. You should include some details on why it is difficult to make predictions due to the different factors influencing climate in the UK.

11. Climate change in the UK
1 D – Some species, such as the black grouse, may become extinct.
2 Any two, explained reasons from: more developing countries are in parts of the world that are likely to be badly hit by climate change, e.g. Africa, Asia; developing countries do not have the financial ability to pay for research and prevention methods to limit the impact of climate change; developing countries have less money to spend on repairing damage, health services, etc.

12. Climate change in Bangladesh
1 Answers will depend on the country or region you have studied, but may include: increased temperatures leading to more drought; increased frequency and severity of river flooding; coastal flooding increasing as sea levels rise; increased frequency of extreme weather – tropical storms, snow storms, etc.
2 **Positive** impacts may include: increasing temperatures may increase the length of the growing season, therefore providing more food and more varieties of food; warmer temperatures will make some places easier to live in and attract more tourists etc. improving economies; plants and animals may move into

the area as climate changes; less heating needed so bills will improve etc. **Negative** impacts may include: increasing river and coastal flooding so people's homes and businesses will be lost/damaged and insurance will increase; increasing frequency and severity of extreme weather events, again damaging property and injuring/killing people; increasing temperatures will bring more tropical diseases to some parts of the world which currently don't have them; increasing frequency of drought will make growing crops and farming more difficult in some places where it is hard already; some plants and animals that can't adapt will become extinct or they'll be lost from some areas as they move to cooler areas, which means the people depending on them will be affected.

Battle for the biosphere

13. Distribution of biomes
1 C – Deciduous forest.
2 Tundra is located at very high latitudes, within the Arctic Circle.

14. A life-support system
1 Meat and fruit.
2 Any two from: the biosphere provides the tools that are essential for human survival, i.e. food and water; provides lots of goods that humans use for products, energy etc.; supports the plants and animals that humans depend on.

15. Threats to the biosphere
1 The destruction of an ecosystem (flora and fauna) of a local environment.
2 One from: harvesting of timber for fuel, building, furniture; clearance of forest for agriculture; clearance for house building, building of roads / railways, building of power stations; mining and quarrying for minerals.

16. Management of the biosphere
1 One from: international / national / local agreements to ban harmful actions; raising awareness of issues to people and governments; finding alternative ways for local people to make money; people volunteering or being paid by governments to conserve and look after land.
2 International means that several countries sign up to it which should mean it is done on a larger scale than if just one nation were doing it. Also makes people and communities aware of which species are endangered.

17. Factors affecting biomes
1 Because the UK's weather usually comes from the west, over the Atlantic, and rain gets dumped on the hills and mountains of the west and on the Pennines (relief rain), so by the time air currents reach the east they are carrying a lot less water.
2 The higher the altitude, the lower the temperature gets and this will affect the type of plants that can grow there. Also the amount of rain will affect plant growth – there is often more rainfall in higher regions. Height can also combine with aspect – different vegetation will grow on different sides.

18. Biosphere management tensions
1 Economic sustainability means something that continues to generate similar amounts of money without needing lots more money to be put into it.
2 Features include: preventing permanent / long-term damage to an ecosystem by not polluting it, destroying plants, overfishing etc; educating local people to ensure they know why they need to manage the ecosystem in which they live for their own benefit and how to manage it, for example by teaching them sustainable farming methods that will not exhaust the ecosystem; helping local people benefit from their ecosystem both socially and economically without damaging it environmentally, for example by helping them irrigate the land better to produce more crops to sell and eat and keep the soil nourished or by helping them make a living through environmental tourism which can help conserve an environment whilst economically benefiting local people.

Water world

19. The hydrological cycle
1 Deforestation would decrease interception, increase surface run-off and infiltration would decrease.
2 Glaciers, oceans, groundwater, lakes.

20. Climate and water supplies
1 Any two from: there may be distinct wet and dry seasons; weather cycles can occur over a number of years, so an area may get 3 or 5 dry years followed by the same number of wet years; there is evidence of global warming and so a rise in temperatures year on year.
2 Your answer should include the following points.
   • A warmer climate in some parts of the world will increase evaporation, leading to increased rainfall and less water in water storage.
   • A warmer climate will also increase the melt from glaciers and ice caps which may lead to flooding in some parts of the world (e.g. Asia) but will also lead to less fresh water supply in the longer term. Also, melting glaciers and ice caps will increase the amount of water stored in the oceans (one of the reasons why climate change will lead to low-lying islands and land areas being submerged).

21. Threats to the hydrological cycle
1 Your answer could include the following causes:
   • untreated sewage pumped into rivers
   • farmers using too much fertiliser and other chemicals in their intensive agriculture which can run off into rivers
   • factories pumping waste products such as chemicals into rivers.
2 They can kill wildlife through suffocation or eating the bag; they pollute the water; they block water pipes.

22. Large-scale water management 1
1 C – aquifer.
2 Any of the following: to regulate the flow of water; to store water for use (e.g. for irrigation) when there are shortages – provides a constant supply; to prevent flooding in times of excess water; to provide a clean supply of water for drinking / washing, etc. which can be piped to homes and businesses over a large area; to generate hydroelectricity; to create an area for water recreation on the reservoirs and lakes created – boating, water skiing, etc.

23. Large-scale water management 2
1 Up to six from: good farmland has been lost by the rising water of the lakes; over 1.3 million people were forced to move their homes away from the rising water of the lake; important cultural and archaeological sites were lost under the lake; there is an increased risk of landslides in some places; the project was very expensive ($US 22.5 billion); sediments are building up behind the dam; downstream areas may become more liable to flooding because the sediment to maintain river banks does not get past the dam (sediment starvation); wetlands have been destroyed.
2 Sediment is trapped behind the dam so sediment does not reach downstream areas and river banks to contain flood waters do not get rebuilt by the sediment.

24. Small-scale water management
1 The following methods improve both the volume / amount and quality of the water (answers from any two).
   • Water harvesting means water is collected in barrels when it rains and stored there to be used in times of drought – improves water supply and quality as the water stays clean.
   • Digging wells to reach water deep underground means water can be accessed even in times when there has been little rain. If they are lined with concrete and have a lid, the water is also kept clean from sewage.
   • Hand pumps can be used to pump water up from deep underground. There is also less chance of water being contaminated so water quality is improved.

2 Any two methods that are explained (answers from any two).
- Wells are dug to reach water. The wells have to be lined with concrete and have a concrete lid to prevent pollution by sewage water.
- Hand pumps are a better way to raise water then using a rope and a bucket.
- Water barrels allow water to be stored and used in times of drought.

Coastal change and conflict

25. Coastal landforms and erosion

1 Your answer should include the following processes.
- Hydraulic action: the force of the wave hitting the rock often forces pockets of air into cracks in the cliff. This air helps to break up the rock.
- Abrasion: the waves pick up stones and hurl these against the cliff and this wears away the rock.
- Attrition: the pebbles carried by the waves themselves get rounder and smaller as they are hurled against the cliffs and bash against each other.

2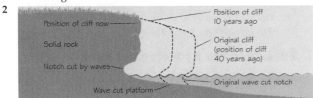

Wave-cut platform formation:
- erosion by waves on a coast forms a notch at the base of the cliff
- as the notch gets bigger, the cliff is undercut
- the cliff collapses
- debris is washed away by the sea and a wave-cut platform is exposed.

26. Coastal landforms and deposition

1 Sand is moved along the shore by longshore drift. At a bend in the coast, drift deposits material and over time sand builds up. A curved end develops due to strong winds and waves.

2 Constructive waves happen in calm conditions when there is little wind. Waves are small and weak with a low frequency – they have a long wavelength. They have a strong swash which deposits material at the coastline but a weak backwash so they do not take much material away, allowing a beach to be built up.

27. Geology of coasts

1 Headlands and bays.

2 Hard rock coasts are resistant to erosion by the sea. An example is Land's End in Cornwall where the cliffs are granite. Here the cliffs are very high, steep and rugged. The cliff face is bare and there are rocks and boulders which have fallen lying at the foot of the cliffs. In comparison, soft rock coasts are quickly and easily eroded by the sea. An example is Holderness in Yorkshire. Here the cliffs are quite high but are less steep and rugged. There are no rocks at the foot of the cliffs, just mud and clay. At Holderness, the soft rock means that the cliffs are retreating rapidly. In comparison, the cliffs in Cornwall are eroding at a very slow rate. However, where there are weaknesses in the hard rock, some erosion features such as caves, arches and stacks have formed. Try to explain your points well and use specific examples to support what you are saying. Make sure that your spelling, punctuation and grammar are really good, that your answer is well-organised and aim to use geographical terminology accurately where possible.

28. Factors affecting coastlines

1 Some depositional features such as spits and bars may be submerged or destroyed by the rising sea levels and increased storms that are expected with climate change. Some depositional features such as beaches may be eroded more quickly as destructive waves and longshore drift takes the material away from the coastline.

2 Any two from:
- property falling into the sea – meaning people lose their homes and businesses which has a big economic and social impact
- loss of land to the sea – again meaning an economic loss of farmland but also potential loss of wildlife habitats and ecosystems
- may negatively impact on tourism as sights, accommodation and features disappear into the sea.

29. Coastal management

1 Any four **advantages** from: protects cliffs; prevents sea removing sand and beach; rocks in riprap absorb wave energy; waves break offshore; can create tourist features, e.g. promenade.
Any four **disadvantages** from: expensive; some hard engineering looks ugly; reefs may interfere with fishing boats; may cause problems further along the coastline.
Make sure that your spelling, punctuation and grammar are really good, that your answer is well-organised and aim to use geographical terminology accurately where possible.

2 Any two from: beach nourishment, managed retreat, cliff regrading.

30. Rapid coastal retreat

Reasons **for** managing the coast (any three from): to prevent people losing their homes; to prevent people losing their businesses; to prevent loss of wildlife habitats; to prevent loss of transport links (e.g. roads and rail lines).
Reasons **against** managing the coast (any 3 from): building sea defences will be very expensive; management may not be sustainable; building sea defences may make problems worse elsewhere; building sea defences may damage the environment.
Make sure that your spelling, punctuation and grammar are really good, that your answer is well-organised and aim to use geographical terminology accurately where possible.

River processes and pressures

31. River systems

1 The **gradient** is steep in the upper course, less steep in the middle and finally gentle in the lower course. The volume of water (**discharge**) in the river is small in the upper course, slightly larger in the middle course and even larger in the lower course.

2 The river **depth** is shallow in the upper course, then the river becomes deeper in the middle section when tributaries join it and even deeper in the lower course as it nears the sea. **Channel shape** in the upper course is narrow floor and steep sides as the river is cutting down faster than the rate at which weathering and mass movement can affect the sides. In the middle section, the shape is flat floor and steep sides created by the meanders. In the lower course, the shape is a wide valley with gently sloping sides.

32. Processes shaping rivers

1 Soil creep – as soil slowly moves down the slopes of a valley, the sides become less steep. Slumping – slope slumps down and material moves down slope making the sides less steep.

2 Freeze-thaw depends on rainfall and freezing, which when the water freezes cracks the rock. In contrast, biological weathering is based on tree and plant roots forcing apart cracks in rocks and so breaking the rocks.

33. Upper course landforms

1 One from:
- hydraulic action – force of the water wears the river bed and banks away
- abrasion – material carried by the river wears the river bed and banks away
- attrition – material carried in the river erodes to become rounder and smaller
- corrosion – rocks and minerals are dissolved by river water.

2 The River Greta flows through resistant limestone and falls 10 metres onto softer, more easily eroded mudstones and this is the plunge pool. This is an area of deeper water which has been created by the rapid erosion of the mudstones. The river is able to erode these softer mudstones quickly. The river waters swirl around and erode the rock into a deep pool.

34. Lower course landforms

1 Deposition is the main process in the lower course of a river because the river is carrying a huge load of material, creating landforms such as ox-bow lakes, floodplains and levées. There is little downward erosion at this stage as the gradient is very gentle.
2 Slip-off slope formation:
   - the river meanders
   - the inside edge of a meander has a slower current so deposition takes place
   - this creates a gently sloping bank called a slip-off slope.

35. Causes and impact of flooding

Any named example will do. For Tewkesbury 2007:
- very heavy rainfall over a short period of time
- this followed days of rain so ground was already waterlogged
- Tewkesbury is fairly flat and lies right next to the mid to lower course of the River Severn so discharge is normally high.

Try to explain your points well and use specific examples to support what you are saying. Make sure that your spelling, punctuation and grammar are really good, that your answer is well-organised and aim to use geographical terminology accurately where possible.

36. Managing river floods

Any three **advantages** from:
- washlands are left without development and this gives the flood water somewhere to go
- trees are planted to help take water out of the soil and reduce water reaching the river
- planners can prevent development of houses and offices on floodplains where rivers may flood
- flood warning systems help to prepare people for floods.

Any three **disadvantages** from:
- using washlands means that the land cannot be used for houses, factories or farming on a full year basis (can be used as 'wet meadow' in dry periods)
- planting trees means the land cannot be used for houses or offices
- planners can prevent development but this may not be the best use of this land
- flood warning systems do not always give much notice.

Try to explain your points well and use specific examples to support what you are saying. Make sure that your spelling, punctuation and grammar are really good, that your answer is well-organised and aim to use geographical terminology accurately where possible.

Oceans on the edge

37. Threats to the ocean

The web of organisms that live in the sea, or an area of the sea.

38. Ecosystem change

Mangrove swamps are an example of a marine ecosystem. They are found near the coast in tropical and subtropical parts of the world and contain many species of plant specially adapted to growing in salty conditions and dealing with tides. They provide a unique ecosystem so are worth looking after.

Mangroves protect the coast from storm surges and tsunamis as they slow down waves. Getting rid of them means putting the coastline, and the humans who live there, at risk. For example, in the Asian tsunami of 2004, the destruction of mangroves for prawn farms and tourist resorts contributed to much of the damage and loss of life in Phuket in Thailand.

Mangrove swamps provide an important food supply for lots of marine and other wildlife including crocodiles, deer and snakes. They also provide shelter for fish and shellfish. The destruction of the mangroves means the loss of habitat for many animals, birds and fish. Fewer fish and shellfish means the fishing industry is affected and the tourist industry could be affected if there is no wildlife to look at. In addition, like all plants, mangroves trap carbon dioxide from the atmosphere so help combat climate change.

39. Pressure on the ecosystem

1 The number of shark would also decline because their food supply would decrease – their food supply, especially tuna and snapper, link back in the chain to phytoplankton.
2 One from: overfishing impacts on organisms both above and below them in the food chain – the organism dependent on the fish being overfished would decline as there would be less food but the organisms the fish being overfished fed on would increase as there would be fewer predators; eutrophication impacts on marine food webs because it leads to over feeding and algal bloom – so some species would massively increase but because this would use up oxygen in the water, other species would die; siltation impacts on marine food webs because silt from soil which has been washed into the seas blocks the sunlight to plants and they die, meaning the species that feed on them decline too.

40. Localised pressures

Population increase near a coastal marine ecosystem adds pressure to all existing human pressures – more people wanting to use ecosystem resources in different ways, e.g. fishing; more sewage output which may be dumped into the sea; more run-off of fertilisers from the land leading to eutrophication pressures; deforestation or other causes of soil erosion could lead to increased siltation; that kind of thing.

41. Local sustainable management

1 This will depend on the case studies used. For the ones in this book, the Coral Triangle seems more sustainable as the Shetland Islands management has created an artificial ecosystem that in itself has some threats to the natural ecosystem of the area (for example, antibiotics and pesticides have been used to control farmed fish diseases, and these chemicals have escaped into the natural ecosystem too). But the Coral Triangle area is very large (6 million km², 120 million people) so it must be very difficult to enforce the species protection laws and fishing controls in practice.
2 See answer to 1. The Shetland Islands has been very successful in employing local people in a real growth industry.

42. Global sustainable management

1 One from: some countries hunt whales for scientific research so continue despite restrictions; whale hunting is a big part of some countries' culture, e.g. Norway and Japan; not all countries sign up to the agreements or stick to them.
2 This will depend on what you have studied but examples include: laws to limit hunting of species, e.g. whales – trying to stop the overfishing of whales to protect the whales themselves and the whole ecosystem, also sturgeon fish, blue-fined tuna; international pollution laws try to limit pollution which damages the organisms that live in the sea; laws on standards of ships to limit probability of accidents leading to pollution such as oil spills.

Try to explain your points well and use specific examples to support what you are saying. Make sure that your spelling, punctuation and grammar are really good, that your answer is well-organised and aim to use geographical terminology accurately where possible.

ANSWERS

Extreme environments

43. Extreme climates: characteristics

1 Less than average rainfall – very arid areas have less than 250 mm per year; often very hot during the day but very cold at night due to lack of cloud cover; no real change throughout the year – no seasons.

2 Very cold throughout the year; little precipitation – mostly snow; glacial areas are covered or partly covered in ice all year round; tundra areas covered in frozen soil. Some seasonal change – short 'spring / summer' growing season in the tundra with long hours of daylight and warmer temperatures, winters extremely cold with few hours of daylight.

44. Why are extreme climates fragile?

1 Small changes in the climate, e.g. in temperature, amount of precipitation, etc. has a huge knock-on effect which can destroy whole ecosystems and / or areas.

2 Small changes in the climate can have catastrophic effects and destroy whole ecosystems and / or areas. You will need to use several examples, explained in detail from: bursting lakes in glacial regions caused by an increase in temperature which can lead to flooding and drown ecosystems; soil melt in tundra regions can lead to solifluction where huge areas of soil move down hill destroying the vegetation (and consequentially the animals and birds it supports); ice melt can lead to loss of hunting ground for predators like polar bears; in hot arid areas, there is always a risk of drought – plants and animals are adapted for living with little water but cannot survive with none at all; desertification increases the arid area so plants and animals that lived in these areas cannot survive. Three additional marks will be awarded for questions like these for spelling, punctuation and grammar so it is important to be careful and try to use as many specialist terms as you can. Try to explain your points well and use specific examples to support what you are saying. Make sure that your spelling, punctuation and grammar are really good, that your answer is well-organised and aim to use geographical terminology accurately where possible.

45. People and extreme climates

1 Money and technology have helped in many ways: better building materials, warmer clothes and buildings, faster and more reliable transport, ability to import a wide range of foodstuffs (which are very expensive to buy, however).

2 Money and technology put pressure on traditional cultures. The cultures usually formed because of the harsh conditions as a way of bringing people together to do the jobs that needed to be done for survival. Some of these traditions remain despite the fact that they are no longer needed for survival, but sometimes in a superficial sort of way or just for tourists. Money has improved transport but many young people use modern transport to leave the harsh living conditions of the polar regions for jobs that earn more money and products that are cheaper to buy, and so these communities often dwindle and die out.

46. Threats to extreme climates

1 Species migration is a possible impact of climate change because animal, plant and bird species are often adapted very closely to a particular temperature range. Changes in global temperature will therefore see some species seeking cooler or warmer conditions.

2 Any one from: increasing temperatures means less ice which means less hunting ground for larger mammals in polar regions, e.g. polar bears, so these species are threatened with extinction; as temperatures increase, vegetation will move north bringing with it animals and birds.

47. Extreme environments: sustainable management

1 D – International treaty to limit climate change.

2 One from: lining wells to avoid contamination by sewage; using hand pumps to get water from deep underground; use barrels to store rainwater for future use.

48. Extreme environments: global management

It is important to include both local actions (which will depend on what you have studied) and global examples (see answers to question 1 above) to gain good marks here. Three additional marks will be awarded for questions like this for spelling, punctuation and grammar so it is important to be careful and to use as many specialist terms as you can.

Try to explain your points well and use specific examples to support what you are saying. Make sure that your spelling, punctuation and grammar are really good, that your answer is well-organised and aim to use geographical terminology accurately where possible.

UNIT 2: PEOPLE AND THE PLANET

Population dynamics

49. World population growth

1 Any four from: more older people; fewer babies; fewer people to work to keep the older people; fewer children in nurseries and primary schools; fewer midwives.

2 Stage 1 features include:
   • a very high birth rate
   • there is also a high death rate
   • both birth and death rates vary a lot from year to year.

50. Population and development

Stage 4 because birth rate is low, death rate is low, high life expectancy with fluctuating rate of population growth – maybe moving into stage 5 as there are a high proportion of older adults in the population and death rate may be exceeding birth rate so population will start to decline.

51. Population issues

1 Problems include:
   • fewer working people paying taxes to support a state pension
   • government needs to provide more facilities such as care homes, meals on wheels and to support medical needs of the elderly
   • housing and other facilities may need adapting to cater for needs of the elderly
   • elderly people and their families have to pay for expensive health care
   • social problems such as loneliness and fear of crime
   • more older people having to work for longer so fewer jobs for the young.

2 This is another term for 'ageing population' which means a high proportion of the population (the same as or greater than working population) aged over 65 years.

52. Managing populations

1 A sustainable population is one that (any four, or two developed points from):
   • has the right amount of people for the resources available
   • has enough people of working age to support dependents (both elderly and children)
   • will continue to provide the right amount of people (i.e. not too many or too few young people)
   • can continue without harming the environment so it will continue to provide the resources that are needed
   • provides the people and skills needed to run the services and businesses of the country.

2 **Overpopulation** means a country has more people then can be supported by its resources.
   Underpopulation means a country has more resources then people.

53. Pro- and anti-natal policies

1 D – encourage people to have more children.

2 Any suitable example could be used but assuming China's one-child policy is chosen, the answer should include ways in which the policy gives benefits to those who have only one child and penalises those that have more:
   • incentives for just having one child, including cash bonuses, long maternity leave (for one child only), good childcare, preferential access to housing

- easy access and education on contraception
- encouraging sterilisation for people who have had one child and forced sterilisation for people who have had more than one child
- penalties / discrimination for having more than one child – poorer housing, childcare, higher taxes, etc.
- female health workers – 'granny police' who monitor the situation of couples
- pressure for abortion of 'non-approved' pregnancies.

54. Migration policies

1 Skills tests are where people who want to move to a country have to pass a test before they are allowed to migrate. This limits the number of migrants allowed as unskilled people will not be allowed to enter.

2 Your answer should include the following points.
- Encouraging immigration should mean more people move to the country so population should increase.
- Additionally, the most likely migrants are young people who are likely to have children which will also help add to the population.
- These migrants will help with labour and skills shortages to improve the economy and help the country run better.
- Additional working people will also mean more tax for the government which it can spend on services or supporting an ageing population.

Consuming resources

55. Types of resources

1 Disadvantages include: all non-renewable resources will eventually run out; many non-renewable resources produce or emit greenhouse gases and contribute to climate change; many are expensive (the rarer the resource, the more expensive it is) which means not everyone can afford them.

2 **Advantages** could include: it is an unlimited supply of energy; minimal carbon emissions; solar panels are getting cheaper to produce and install. **Disadvantages** include: the UK does not get enough sunshine to make it suitable for solar power stations to generate a lot of energy so it can only be used at a small scale (e.g. on individual buildings); it is not constant (especially in winter) so alternative supplies of energy are needed; huge areas of panels are needed to produce a significant amount of energy; panels are quite expensive (although getting cheaper) and they only last about 20 years.

56. Resource supply and use 1

1 Global demand for oil will increase over the next 30 years as the consumption per person rises, especially in developing countries where there is a growing demand for cars, housing and oil-fueled technology.

2 Global economic growth will mean that more people will want cars, air conditioning in their homes, more housing and technology. This will put more pressure on global energy supplies but countries will begin to export less as they try to conserve their non-renewable resources for their own use. This could lead to conflict between countries over supplies of gas and oil.

57. Resource supply and use 2

1 Generally, more developed countries consume a lot more resources than less developed countries; inequalities in resource supply is less pronounced.

2 Any two from: ability of consumers to pay for it; lifestyle (e.g. the car is more important in come countries than others); availability of the resource in that country; more developed countries likely to use more resources generally than less developed ones – more use of technology, etc.

58. Consumption theories

1 Malthus thought food production would not rise at the same rate as population growth so famines would occur, whereas Boserup thought more people would find new ways to increase food production and would match demand.

2 Supply means how much of a resource is available and how easy it is to get it, whereas consumption means how much of the resource is used by people.

59. Managing consumption

1 Ways include: reducing the volume of toilet flushes (this is where most water gets wasted); fixing any dripping taps; reducing the shut off time of automatic taps if they are fitted; altering any garden areas to drought-tolerant plant species; fitting water butts to collect and store water from rainwater run-off; regular checking of water meters to report on the success of water-saving methods and spot any leaks; educate people to turn off taps when they brush their teeth and take less time in the shower.

2 National level includes: educational awareness campaigns to try and make people alter their habits; setting school curriculum so children learn about reducing resource consumption; setting laws and fining companies who produce lots of waste or do not recycle; provide grants and subsidies for home insulation, renewable energy supplies and more efficient boilers. Local level includes: organising recycling and composting collections and centres; small leaflet campaigns to encourage people to recycle.

60. Potential of renewables

1 Renewable energy will not run out so there will be a continual supply of the resource. At the moment, the world uses only a small percentage of renewable so is more dependant on resources which are getting smaller and will eventually run out.

2 Reducing consumption involves interfering with the way people want to live their lives. In developing countries, people want the same as what people have in developed countries, so reducing consumption can be difficult if there are no transport or energy alternatives available. Switching to alternative or renewable resources is very expensive and can involve upsetting a lot of people (e.g. residents near wind farms).

Globalisation

61. Changing employment patterns

1 A – It shows how the employment structure of a country changes as it develops.

2 Any three from: another sector called the quaternary sector now grows to be more important; this is based on research and development; it is also based on information technology; research provides expertise to discover new products and services.

62. Employment sectors

1 Your answer should include the following points.
- LICs: primary sector is hugely important – employs the vast majority of people. Most are subsistence farmers and not paid for their work.
- MICs: primary sector is less important than LICs but still large. Likely to include mining and quarrying as well as agriculture and fishing.
- HICs: primary sector is unimportant – employs very few people due to mechanisation as well as reduction in this type of industry.

2 Working conditions in the manufacturing and construction industries of middle-income countries are likely to be poor, even unsafe, due to lack of regulation. Hours of work are long but pay is quite good (although low by developed world standards).

63. Impact of globalisation

1 Countries such as China and India which manufacture and sell goods, and buy raw materials and food. These areas have cheap labour and a good infrastructure of roads and railways. These countries get quite good prices for their manufactured goods because of the cheap labour but they have to buy expensive services usually from HICs because there are relatively few providers of these services internally.

2 The World Trade Organization (WTO) aims to encourage more and more trade between countries and has been working since 1995. Its purpose is to make trade as free from things like import duties as possible. This should benefit all countries involved in trade. So trade is truly global.

64. International trade and capital flows

1 FDI is investment from one country to another, usually done by a TNC. It involves buying businesses, land or facilities in another country to take advantage of cheap labour, gain access to foreign markets or gain resources. It usually benefits both countries but the 'home' country of the TNC benefits far more than the country receiving the investment.

2 One from the following reasons.
- There have been a series of agreements between countries and between trading blocks (like the European Union) which allows easier movement of goods and services between countries.
- Containerisation has allowed the development of complex, long-distance trade. Containers have also reduced the cost of international transport.
- There has been a revolution in IT through email, text, fax and phone which was made possible by communication satellites and undersea fibre-optic cables meaning people can communicate over long distances very quickly.
- Faster and cheaper transport, e.g. the growth of air transport for both people, raw materials and end products.
- The growth of TNCs which trade between themselves and with each other.
- The work of the International Monetary Fund (IMF) in making it easier to invest in other countries.

65. TNCs: secondary sector

1 Any two from: rates of pay for workers remain low; working conditions may be poor; (especially in secondary sector) likely to create pollution (air and water); although employment will be provided, little profit will be generated for the developing country.

2 The answer will depend on your chosen TNC but may include points similar to the following.
- People in developing countries have lower wages than in the UK so TNCs can make bigger profits from using labour there to make their products.
- Land for factories and offices is cheaper in developing countries – reducing costs.
- In Asia there is a huge, skilled labour force.
- Many TNCs sell their products in Asia too, so locating factories there means they are closer to the Asian markets.
- Fewer health and safety laws and regulations for workers mean workers can work long hours and less money is needed to spend on working conditions.

66. TNCs: tertiary sector

1 The answer will depend on your chosen TNC. Think about what sector the TNC operates in, where their headquarters, retail outlets or manufacturing facilities are located. Does it manufacture its own products? Does it use third parties? Where are these located? If it manufactures its own products where does this take place, where does it source its materials? Think about the number of people employed directly and indirectly and in which locations.

2 See answer to question 1 above. In addition: these stores sell some of the same products but also some 'local' ones, specific to the country or region where the store is located. Huge spread of stores means that the business is protected, for example, from economic problems in one region or country. Also, operates in a huge number of different markets – food, finance, clothing, etc. – which again helps it maximise profit and protect business as a whole.

Development dilemmas

67. What is development?

1 At least two of the following: economic measures show average figures only so they do not show how wealth is distributed within a country; economic data is not always accurate and does not include non-official measures such as the cash economy which is large in many LEDCs; economic measures do not give any indication of what that wealth is spent on; people consider other indicators – human, social and political indicators – as just as important as wealth in measuring the development in a country or region.

2 GDP is just the Gross Domestic Product where as GDP per capita is the GDP split by the total population. This gives a much clearer indicator – for example, China has a huge GDP but a much smaller GDP per capita because it earns a lot of money but there is a massive population.

68. The development gap

1 B – People's quality of life.

2 The difference between the most and least developed countries.

69. Development

Your answer will depend on the example chosen. For Rwanda: from 1980 to 1985, development was very slow but after 1985, it took a backward step. After the outbreak of civil war in 1990, stagnation increased until it reached a new low after the genocide of 1994. Between 1995 and 2000, there were small improvements and since 2000, Rwanda has continued to develop.

70. Theories of development

1 Any two from: it is out of date; it is based on the development of European countries when conditions were very different in the 18th and 19th centuries; it assumes all countries start from the same place; it does not take into account any variables of a country's resources, population or climate hazard; it only sees a continuous growth cycle – some countries have stalled at a certain stage.

2 Dependency theory says that richer states exploit poorer ones – they do not benefit from capitalism because the rules are set by the most developed countries which can set trade restrictions, loan money but with big interest rates and conditions attached, etc.

71. Regional disparity

1 The difference in economic development between different areas within the same country.

2 Any two from: people in poorer areas are likely to have a lower quality of life than those in richer areas; conflict / tensions could erupt between different areas; people are likely to move away from the poorer areas leaving these areas to get poorer; people are likely to move into richer areas potentially causing overcrowding, unemployment, etc.; the development of the whole country will be slowed down by the periphery.

72. Types of development

Answer depends on your named example, but for the Madeira River Scheme, **advantages** include: the dam will produce 3150 MW of electricity – cheap, clean energy; develop a peripheral region of Brazil; is creating thousands of jobs; involves building new roads that will improve communications in the region. **Disadvantages** include: it is very costly, $5.5 billion; it disrupts fishing, and many thousands of local people rely on fishing to make a living; new roads will open up the region to more soy farming, which means clearance of tropical rainforest.

The changing economy of the UK

73. Industrial change in the UK

Two from: companies have invested more money in research and development to develop new products; new technologies (e.g. smartphones, sat navs, tablet computers) have meant that IT companies have grown hugely; the public sector (e.g. universities and government departments) have invested more in R&D.

74. UK employment

For **staff**, flexible working and they still earn a wage. For **employer**, saves money.

75. UK regions and employment

1 Any two contrasting regions could be used. For South East and North East England, you should include the following points.
- North East England has higher unemployment than the South East – due to the decline of traditional industries (e.g. iron and steel production, shipbuilding) and automation within other industries (e.g. chemicals). The South East had much less traditional industry.

- South East England has some locational advantages for certain industries – it is close to the capital city, London, and has easy access to Europe so it is ideally placed for tertiary employment such as financial services and service industries such as health. Some businesses see the North East as 'too far away'.
- Many educated people migrate to the South East / London from other parts of the UK (and the world) because there are better job opportunities which in turn attracts businesses to this area rather than the North East.
- Government has tried to address the balance by relocating some government departments in the North East – in recent years this has added to unemployment due to government cuts.
- South East England is the focus of UK transport links so firms, particularly light industries (e.g. electronic), want to locate here as costs for transporting materials plus final products will be cheaper.
- Proximity to the North Sea means that the North East has many people employed in the oil and gas industries – however, the largest oil refinery in the UK is located in the South East (Southampton) due to its location to the rest of the world.
- Some parts of the North East have become 'niche' centres, e.g. Tyneside for stem cell research, Sunderland for science and high-tech industries – firms have chosen to locate here because of cheaper land / buildings.

Try to explain your points well and use specific examples to support what you are saying. Make sure that your spelling, punctuation and grammar are really good, that your answer is well-organised and aim to use geographical terminology accurately where possible.

2 Any region could be used. For South East England, any two from:
- large, well-educated workforce for businesses and services to employ
- very large market for selling goods to – wealthy region too so many of these have high incomes
- proximity to London – the power and decision-making base of the UK, which is where most companies HQs are located
- proximity to Europe via Channel tunnel– easy to transport people, raw materials and products
- good transport links to the rest of the world – several international airports and ports
- government actions – grants, etc. – have moved the location of some offices in the 1970s out of central London to other towns and cities in the South East.

76. Environmental impact of changing employment

Your answer will depend on the area you have studied. For Sandwell, West Midlands, you should include the following points.
- In the 1990s, The Black Country Development Corporation and Tipton Challenge helped to improve conditions. These were paid for by central and local government.
- Similarly, Sandwell had one of 21 Urban Regeneration Companies from 2003 who helped to reclaim land and attract new investment. This attracted new industries, such as the Automotive Component Park, which in turn created new jobs.
- The New Deal for Communities programme helped improve housing and facilities up to 2010.
- Housing Market Renewal Pathfind Areas – 15-year regeneration problem which aims to improve neighbourhoods.
- Sandwell Council is reducing its contribution to climate change by reducing emissions by 27% and by 2018 should have reduced them by 45%.
- British Trust for Conservation Volunteers – has created new green spaces.
- 45 km of new road were built.
- New primary schools have been built and high schools refurbished.

Try to explain your points well and use specific examples to support what you are saying. Make sure that your spelling, punctuation and grammar are really good, that your answer is well-organised and aim to use geographical terminology accurately where possible.

77. Greenfield and brownfield development

1 D – Land that has not been developed before.
2 Your answer will depend on which sites you have studied at school.
At Longbridge in Birmingham, 2000 new homes will be built on a 468-acre site of a former car plant. Bournville College has relocated there to a new £66 million facility. Three new green parks are being created. 10 000 new jobs will eventually be created. There will be a new local centre with 25 shops including a large Sainsbury's supermarket and community facilities (My Place youth centre). Shop owners in nearby Northfield will lose a lot of trade and some have already closed. The development eases pressure on the nearby green belt. Local house prices are already rising as the development grows. Local people may no longer be able to afford them.
Try to explain your points well and use specific examples to support what you are saying. Make sure that your spelling, punctuation and grammar are really good, that your answer is well-organised and aim to use geographical terminology accurately where possible. Use phrases such as 'whereas' to help you compare.

78. New employment areas

1 Any one from the following.
- The UK is committed to reducing greenhouse gas emissions so more renewable energy sources (e.g. wind or water) need to be used, creating new jobs in building and running these new power plants.
- Likely to be a growth in greener transport, which will mean more jobs in this area.
- As UK businesses and households try to become more sustainable, there is likely to be an increase in jobs in waste and water management.
2 Advances in the digital sector are increasingly important to the UK economy because individuals and companies will rely more and more on IT technology. More employees will be needed in creating and developing new products and other employees will be needed for training, maintenance and repair of existing products. Jobs in the digital economy will also become more important to the UK as jobs in other industries and services decline – partly due to mechanisation driven by digital technology taking over people's former roles.

Changing settlements in the UK

79. Urban change in the UK

1 The opposite of industrialisation – the decrease in heavy industry such as iron and steel production, shipbuilding, etc.
2 Any one from: increased population means more people so urban areas have grown as more housing, businesses and services have been needed; movement of people away from inner city areas to the suburbs and rural-urban fringe (and even out of urban areas altogether); migration within the UK to places of economic growth – especially growth of London; different age groups migrating to different urban areas – young people closer to the centre, families and older people in the suburbs, retirement migration to rural areas, etc.

80. Changes in urban areas

1 Deprivation means an area which is lacking in things necessary for people to lead healthy lives. Factors which contribute to an area being classed as 'deprived' include: poor and overcrowded housing, lack of amenities and services, lack of jobs and educational opportunities.
2 Any one from: there is more space so people can build bigger houses with large gardens, outbuildings, garages, etc.; wealthier people can afford to commute further distances to work; wealthier people can afford the recreational facilities that are close by.

81. Rural settlements

1 C – Remote upland villages.
2 Any one from: people want to live closer to countryside; house prices are cheaper; usually more open space; transport has improved so it is easier to travel to work over further distances; seen as 'safer' and nicer place to live than in more urban areas.

82. Contrasting rural areas

1 Any one from: lack of employment diversity or opportunity; lack of access to leisure and entertainment; few services; bad transport links; media making urban areas look more exciting.

2 This will depend on the areas you have studied, but for the ones mentioned here (North Wiltshire and Scottish Highlands): both have beautiful landscapes that people enjoy; Wiltshire is far more accessible than the Scottish Highlands though – some areas extremely remote; location means that access to services in Wiltshire is generally better as you have to travel further in the Highlands; better job opportunities in Wiltshire because of its location and good transport links to urban areas; climate and landscape of the Highlands restricts the jobs available too – only really sheep farming, forestry, tourism, etc.; increasing population of Wiltshire means it is becoming less rural though – pressure on services and housing; Highlands are more affordable and do not generally have a housing shortage. This is a SPAG question so note that your spelling, punctuation and grammar will be taken into account – try to use as many specialist terms as you can remember.

83. Impact of housing demand

1 Urban regeneration means improving urban areas – growing them through improving services, housing and the economy of the area.

2 Any one from: improvements to residents' housing; building new housing; providing new job opportunities through growth of businesses and services; improving service provision; improving physical environment making it a more pleasant area; improving transport links.

84. Making rural areas sustainable

Any one from: giving loans, grants and advice to small businesses to help boost the economy and create jobs; creating tourist facilities to encourage people to visit; providing training and education for rural jobs; building / providing affordable housing (very little of this has been done!); improving rural communications – broadband, mobile phone masts, etc.

The challenges of an urban world

85. Global trends in urbanisation

In the developed world, towns and cities grew in the 19th century during the Industrial Revolution. There was an Agricultural Revolution at the same time so new machinery meant fewer farm workers were needed. So people moved to towns where there were jobs in new factories. These are push factors just as in modern developing cities. Towns grew at rates of 10% per year; growth in developing cities is much faster (23%). Growth in developed countries was over a much longer period of time than is currently the situation in developing cities. Urban growth on a world scale is now heavily focused on developing countries. So the speed of urbanisation in developing countries is much faster then in 19th-century Europe. The main reasons for the growth of cities in developing countries are due to natural increase (birth rates higher than death rates) because of high fertility rates (large numbers of children per woman). So cities are dominated by young children. Natural increase did play a part in the growth of developed cities but not as important as in developing cities today. Pull factors were similar – jobs and services.

Try to explain your points well and use specific examples to support what you are saying. Make sure that your spelling, punctuation and grammar are really good, that your answer is well-organised and aim to use geographical terminology accurately where possible. Use comparison phrases such as 'whereas' to help you compare.

86. Megacities

Megacities in the developing world (e.g. Mexico City) have a large proportion of young people because there are high fertility rates. In contrast, megacities in the developed world (e.g. Osaka) have a large proportion of older people because fertility rates are much lower and life expectancy is longer.

87. Urban challenges: developed world

1 Large eco-footprints are the result of cities in the developed world using large amounts of resources such as fuels, water and food, and when they create waste and pollution and do not recycle much. York has quite high levels of recycling but London, for example, has lower levels of recycling. Low levels of recycling mean that more waste is going to landfill and this is expensive. Traffic generates air pollution which again makes for a larger eco-footprint.

2 Your answer should include some of the following points.
- Provide food for its population – far less food is grown in cities so it needs to be transported in, which costs money and energy in terms of transport and packaging and means the price of food is expensive.
- Provide water for its population – demand for water is greater than the supply available. Lifestyle – appliances and single living – means huge amounts of water being used which is not sustainable. Cities usually positioned a long way from where water is stored.
- Coping with rising energy demands – most energy at the moment is from fossil fuels which add to CO_2 emissions. These sources will also run out. Current usage is not sustainable – alternative sources have to be used and people and businesses need to use less. Rising cost of energy is an increasing problem for the poorest in developed countries.
- Congestion and pollution caused by transport, mostly private cars. Getting people around the city quickly and without causing pollution is a major problem.
- Dealing with waste is very expensive and landfill sites are unsustainable. Recycling and reducing waste need to be encouraged.

Try to explain your points well and use specific examples to support what you are saying. Make sure that your spelling, punctuation and grammar are really good, that your answer is well-organised and aim to use geographical terminology accurately where possible.

88. Urban challenges: developing world

1 D – Selling goods found on rubbish tips.

2 Any one from the following points.
- Traffic congestion is very bad in cities like Mexico City and Beijing. Here large numbers of vehicles have poor exhaust systems which generate serious air pollution creating health risks such as asthma and bronchitis. In some cases, dense smog is created covering the whole area of Mexico City.
- Water pollution is widespread because rivers and seas are used as dustbins to get rid of waste. This destroys wildlife and makes water unsafe for drinking.
- Sewage can get into water supplies, especially in shanty towns, making the water unsafe to drink.

89. Reducing York's eco-footprint

Two for **people** from: people would use less energy; lower power bills; reduced water bills and water consumption.
Two for the **environment** from: less carbon dioxide in the atmosphere; less global warming; fewer violent storms or droughts.

90. Strategies in the developing world

Any suitable example could be used, for example Curitiba, Brazil.
- Public transport is very successful – used by 85% of the population. The buses run in central lanes and are interconnected through 20 terminals. The system is fast, cheap and efficient. The buses run very frequently, some every 90 seconds. The system transports 2.6 million people each day so has helped improve people's lives and the buses use alternative fuels such as natural gas which creates less pollution (good for people's health as well as the environment).
- The city has preserved its green areas, with 28 parks and wooded areas making the environment more attractive for people. Builders get tax rebates if their projects include green space and new lakes now absorb flood waters which were a problem in the past.

- People living in low-income areas bring their rubbish bags to centres where they swap them for bus tickets and food. So there is less litter and less disease.
- Children can exchange recycled waste for school supplies, food and chocolate – reducing waste (less litter and disease) as well as helping education.

Try to explain your points well and use specific examples to support what you are saying. Make sure that your spelling, punctuation and grammar are really good, that your answer is well-organised and aim to use geographical terminology accurately where possible.

The challenges of a rural world

91. Rural economies

1 C – Roses.
2 Commercial farming is where the vast majority of produce is sold for profit rather than personal consumption. Cash crops are an example.

92. Rural challenges: developed world

1 A honeypot location is a tourist attraction that gets loads of visitors while the surrounding area does not get as many. It might be because it is a particularly beautiful area or something with a special landscape feature or historic landmark or a link to a film or TV. One example of a honeypot location is Bourton-on-the-Water in the Cotswold region of Gloucestershire. It is a very picturesque village but becomes extremely crowded in summer when coaches of tourists come to visit. What example did you put and how did you link it to your honeypot definition?
2 Second homes can cause problems because they push up house prices meaning that local people who live and work in rural areas all the time cannot afford to buy a house. Second homes are only lived in during weekends and / or holidays so the people using them don't need to use some local services such as shops very often or other local services such as schools at all which means rural services have fewer customers and have to close. They can also add to feelings of isolation for people who live in rural areas all the time as there are fewer people around.

93. Rural challenges: developing world

1 Leads to depopulation and ageing population in rural areas. Often the people who leave rural areas for urban ones in developing countries are young men – the very people most needed to farm the land so may lead to food shortages, etc. The people left behind are usually the old and young who need people to care for them and who are less able to work. Means less people to run rural services.
2 This will depend on the area chosen but for rural areas of Kenya challenges include: lack of paid jobs – mostly subsistence farming; HIV / AIDs leading to rising death rates in the working population so fewer people to run services and grow food; large commercial farms take the best land and export the food overseas so local people see little benefit and are left with the poorest land; land degradation in some areas means farming yields are poor; struggles over land ownership and poor farming techniques also lead to low crop yields; tourism brings income but much of this goes to large companies rather than local people and also means local people cannot use the land for farming, etc.; rural-urban migration of mostly young men has led to an ageing population in rural areas which has in turn led to lower crop yields, lack of people to run services, lack of people to look after the elderly.
Try to explain your points well and use specific examples to support what you are saying. Make sure that your spelling, punctuation and grammar are really good, that your answer is well-organised and aim to use geographical terminology accurately where possible.

94. Rural development projects

1 Any one from: access to education for children; access to education and training for businesses (including farming); access to health care provision; access to loans and money to improve businesses (for example, through micro-finance); improved access to clean water and good sanitation; improved transport; electricity; improved communications with the rest of the country.
2 Any one from: education for adults and children is vital for improving their chances of getting a paid job and / or starting and running their own businesses; improves knowledge for how to look after children, health care, training for latest farming techniques or how to use equipment so helps to improve the quality of life.

95. Developed world: farming

Examples for **economic sustainability** could include: diversification to make money in different ways and from different products (examples should be given and explained); selling products in different ways (examples should be given and explained); selling or renting the land / buildings for another purpose. Examples for **environmental sustainability** could include: organic farming – not using chemical fertilisers or pesticides; rotating crops so nutrients are put back into the soil; using drip irrigation; replanting hedgerows to prevent loss of topsoil and provide a habitat for wildlife. This is a SPAG question so note that your spelling, punctuation and grammar will be taken into account – try to use as many specialist terms as you can remember.

96. Developing world: farming

Fair trade means producers have a guaranteed minimum income so they are not as susceptible to world markets and earn more money. Fair trade also raises more money to be put back into local communities and farming infrastructure. Workers' conditions and pay generally improve as this is monitored. The environment is checked which helps make it sustainable.

UNIT 3: MAKING GEOGRAPHICAL DECISIONS

99. Looking at sources

B, C

100-101 Section 1: Oil supplies in the USA

Canada has large oil reserves which could be exported to the USA. The USA needs more oil because renewable sources don't supply enough energy to meet demands. However, environmental campaigners are against drilling for oil because it damages the natural wilderness and causes pollution.

102-103 Section 2: Developing new oil resources 1

The main advantages of drilling in the WAR are, firstly, that the Trans-Alaska Pipeline, (see Figure 2a page 101) which was built in the 1970s to carry oil from the North Slope oil field, is already in place so there would be no need to build a new pipeline to take the oil to Valdez. Secondly, the WAR is US territory, so there are no problems with other countries. Thirdly, there is already a route for oil tankers to take oil from Valdez to the rest of the USA.

104-105 Section 3: Developing new oil resources 2

Farmers could switch to crops that need less water, such as sunflowers. Water could be recycled or drip-feed water systems could be used. Farmers could also use terracing and crop rotation to conserve water.

106-107 Section 4: Renewable energy

This form of renewable energy is not as profitable for companies like this, and so they may want to focus on other areas of their business such as oil and gas.

108–109 Options (pages)

1 • You need to give a clear, well-structured answer. There are 3 marks available for SPaG so make sure that you use geographical terminology correctly and that your spelling, punctuation and grammar are really good.

• Aim to describe at least two advantages using evidence from the resource booklet and from your own knowledge of Units 1 and 2 to support your points.

• Option 2: Building the US Keystone XL pipeline. The pipeline would run from the tar sands of Alberta, Canada, to the oil refineries on the US Gulf Coast. This offers several advantages. Canada is a close neighbour of the USA and is a stable, friendly country. Up to 100 000 people would be employed in building and operating the pipeline, and the US states that it will run through will receive extra tax revenues. The USA currently imports 43% of its oil. If the pipeline was built, the tar sands would provide 5% of US oil needs and save 9% of US imports. The pipeline will cost about $7 billion to build but this is cheaper than drilling for oil in the WAR, which costs about $33 billion.

Drilling in the WAR may cause more environmental damage than choosing the pipeline option. The WAR option would lead to the loss of wildlife habitats and wildlife such as the gyrfalcons, and increase global warming. The only real environmental threat of the pipeline would be to the Sandhills of Nebraska – an area of wetland – and some deforestation over the tar sands themselves. The Sandhills area and the Ogallala Aquifer around it could be protected from pollution with the use of sensors on the pipeline to detect any leaks. Although using renewable sources of energy would cause less pollution, they cannot meet the USA's demand for energy. The pipeline option therefore offers lots of benefits to the US and, if carefully monitored, will not damage the wildlife or water supplies although there will be greenhouse gas emissions when the natural gas is burned off during extraction.

2 • You need to give a clear, well-structured answer. There are 3 marks available for SPaG so make sure that you use geographical terminology correctly and that your spelling, punctuation and grammar are really good.

• Justify your choice by describing several positive aspects of your chosen option and support with relevant data. You should also discuss potential drawbacks and alternative options. Make sure you use data from the resource booklet and from your own knowledge from Units 1 and 2.

• Option 1: Drill in the Western Arctic Reserve (WAR). Oil imports are now costing a lot – the world price of oil has increased from about $70 a barrel in 2007 to over $100 a barrel in 2011. Since the USA imports 43% of its oil, it now needs to use its own resources to save money. There are several other advantages, including reducing the USA's dependence on other countries which may become unfriendly. Also, there is already an oil field (North Slope) in place so the technology for drilling in a hostile environment already exists. A Trans-Alaska pipeline also exists and can be used to carry the oil to the port of Valdez and then tankers can use the existing route to take it on to the rest of the USA.

There are, however, disadvantages to choosing this option. The main ones are to the environment. The WAR region is home to migrating birds, moose, caribou, falcons, wolves and polar bears. Drilling might destroy many wildlife habitats and may lead to some of these animals becoming endangered or extinct but oil companies have learned a lot about minimising pollution so the threat might not be so bad. Another threat is the increase in global warming that would result from drilling. 40 000 tonnes of oil waste come from each rig and 50 000 tonnes of extra nitrogen dioxide would be released into the atmosphere. But the other option – the US Keystone XL pipeline – may also damage the environment and possibly pollute important water supplies. The pipeline option also means that the USA still has pay to import oil because the oil reserves are in Canada, so the WAR option is better.

There are no questions printed on this page.

There are no questions printed on this page.

There are no questions printed on this page.

There are no questions printed on this page.

There are no questions printed on this page.

Published by Pearson Education Limited, Edinburgh Gate, Harlow, Essex, CM20 2JE.

www.pearsonschoolsandfecolleges.co.uk

Copies of official specifications for all Edexcel qualifications may be found on the Edexcel website: www.edexcel.com

Text and original illustrations © Pearson Education Limited 2013
Edited, produced and typeset by Wearset Ltd, Boldon, Tyne and Wear
Illustrated by Wearset Ltd, Boldon, Tyne and Wear
Cover illustration by Miriam Sturdee

The rights of Rob Bircher, David Flint and Kirsty Taylor to be identified as authors of this work have been asserted by them in accordance with the Copyright, Designs and Patents Act 1988.

First published 2013

16 15 14
10 9 8 7 6 5 4 3 2

British Library Cataloguing in Publication Data
A catalogue record for this book is available from the British Library

ISBN 978 1 446 90537 1

Acknowledgements
The publisher would like to thank the following for their kind permission to reproduce their photographs:

(Key: b-bottom; c-centre; l-left; r-right; t-top)

Alamy Images: Andre Seale 90, Elly Godfroy 95tr, FLPA 95c, GL Archive 58l, imagebroker 102, Izel Photography – EC 81, Jane Tregelles 32, Mark Humphreys 11, Midland Aerial Pictures 76, Mike Kipling Photography 79, Paul Glendell 36br, Peter Alvey 59t, PURPLE MARBLES YORK 1 87, Robert Harding Picture Library Ltd 28, Sami Sarkis (2) 37, Skyscan Photolibrary 26, Steven Hunt 33; **Corbis:** Wendy Stone 93; **Getty Images:** AFP 99, AFP / Findlay Kember 65, Brian Stablyk 104, David Joyner 83, Mario Tama / Staff 72, Matt Cardy 89, Yadid Levy 45r; **Pearson Education Ltd:** Lord and Leverett 51t, Jules Selmes 51c; **Science Photo Library Ltd:** TON KOENE / VISUALS UNLIMITED, INC 15; **Shutterstock.com:** Atlas Pix 29tr, Elzbieta Sekowska 36bl, FAUP 69, George Green 29tl, Igor Koza 29b, lexaarts 64r, PRILL 23; **SuperStock:** NASA / National Geographic 56, Norbert Eisele-Hein / i / imagebroker.net 45l; **Veer/Corbis:** Alexey Stiop 51b, alptraum 21l, 64l, ecopic 44r, George Burba 34, goldenKB 74r, imagix 6, manfredxy 59, Peter Kirillov 44l, phb.cz 22, smontgom65 42, ssuaphoto 98, stefano lunardi 74l, tepic 95l, tomas24 38, toxawww 21r, wayoutwest 36t

All other images © Pearson Education

Picture Research by: Caitlin Swain

We are grateful to the following for permission to reproduce copyright material:
Figures
Figures on page 1 from U.S. Geological Survey; Figure on page 26 adapted from 'The process of Longshore drift', http://geography fieldwork.com/LongshoreDrift.htm, Barcelona Field Studies Centre http://geographyfieldwork.com, Adapted diagram courtesy of Barcelona Field Studies Centre, www.geographyfieldwork.com; Figure on page 31 adapted from Geography and Change, Hodder Arnold (Flint, D., Flint, C. and Punnett, N. 1996); Figure on page 35 adapted from Geography: an integrated approach, Nelson Thornes Ltd (Waugh. 1995); Figure on page 50 from www.census.gov/population/international/data/idb/informationgateway.php, U.S. Census Bureau, International Database; Figure on page 100 from U.S. Energy Information Administration, http://www.eia.gov/dnav/pet/pet_move_impcus_a2_nus_epc0_im0_mbblpd_m.htm; Figure on page 100 from U.S. Energy Information Administration, http://www.eia.gov/forecasts/steo/report/prices.cfm; Figure on page 106 from U.S. Department of Energy, Carbon Dioxide Information Analysis Center

Maps
Map on page 43 from U.S. Geological Survey; Maps on page 57, page 100 from BP Statistical Review of World Energy 2007, http://www.bp.com/liveassets/bp_internet/china/bpchina_english/STAGING/local_assets/downloads_pdfs/statistical_review_of_world_energy_full_review_2008.pdf page 13, Reproduced with permission of BP; Map on page 100 from BP Statistical Review of World Energy 2007, http://www.bp.com/liveassets/bp_internet/china/bpchina_english/STAGING/local_assets/downloads_pdfs/statistical_review_of_world_energy_full_review_2008.pdf page 7, Reproduced with permission of BP

Text
Article on page 106 adapted from Financial Times, BP puts US wind power units up for sale (Ed Crooks), 3 April 2013 http://www.ft.com/cms/s/0/41d4f8ca-9bdd-11e2-8485-00144feabdc0.html#axzz2c8bwtcGj, © The Financial Times Limited. All Rights Reserved.

In some instances we have been unable to trace the owners of copyright material, and we would appreciate any information that would enable us to do so.

Every effort has been made to trace the copyright holders and we apologise in advance for any unintentional omissions. We would be pleased to insert the appropriate acknowledgement in any subsequent edition of this publication.